Stanley Baker

Stanley Baker

A Life in Film

Robert Shail

UNIVERSITY OF WALES PRESS
CARDIFF
2008

www.uwp.co.uk

British Library Cataloguing-in-Publication Data

A catalogue record for this book is available from the British Library.

ISBN 978-0-7083-2126-3

Mixed Sources

Product group from well-managed forests, and other controlled sources

www.fsc.org Cert no. TT-CoC-002424

© 1996 Forest Stewardship Council

The paper used for this book is FSC-certified and totally chlorine-free. FSC (the Forest Stewardship Council) is an international network to promote responsible management of the world's forests.

Printed in Malta by Gutenberg Press Ltd.

For Cerri

Contents

Illustrations

Acknowledgements

In researching this book I have been aided by a large number of people whose generosity and kindness has helped to make this work possible. I would like to thank the staff of the British Film Institute, The National Library of Wales, The National Screen and Sound Archive of Wales, the Rhondda Local Studies Collection at Treorchy Public Library, and the University of Wales, Lampeter. My thanks go to my colleagues in the Department of Film and Media at the University of Wales, Lampeter for their encouragement and support during my absence on study leave. I'm particularly grateful to Steve Gerrard who looked after much of my teaching duties for me.

Following a letter which I sent to *The Rhondda Leader* I was contacted by many people who had known Stanley Baker in his youth in Ferndale. I would like to thank David Williams, Barry Sullivan, Hayden Jones, Huw Evans, Ken Lewis, Tom Condon, Howard Lloyd, Owen Price and Joan Howells for sharing their memories of Stanley with me. A special mention must go to Alwyn Davies and Alun Clement who showed me around Ferndale and introduced me to a number of local people. I have been delighted by the warmth which greeted me from everyone I encountered in the Rhondda; it's easy to understand why it remained such an important place for Stanley Baker.

Others on the roll of honour include my fellow academics Sheldon Hall, David Berry, James Chapman, Val Hill and Gwenno Ffrancon. Also Nick Kelland at Ferndale Library, Ralph Dyer (who runs a website dedicated to Stanley) and Gareth Morse, son of the late Glynne Morse who played such an important part in Stanley's story. I am immensely grateful to Steve Freer at BBC Wales for the invaluable materials he made available to me and to Richard Haylor who supplied a number of useful film magazines.

Special thanks go to Stanley's friend and business partner Bob Porter, to his sons Martin, Glyn and Adam, his cousin John Wyatt and his sister Muriel, and to Gavrik Losey for speaking to me about Stanley. Most importantly, I must thank Lady Ellen Baker who has been unstintingly generous with her time. Her continuing love and appreciation of Stanley are the finest tributes he could have hoped for.

ACKNOWLEDGEMENTS

This book was made possible with the financial support of the Pantyfed-wyn Trust, the University of Wales, Lampeter and the Arts and Humanities Research Council.

Introduction

The first image of Stanley Baker that comes into my mind is that of Lieutenant John Chard in *Zulu* (1964). In his blood-red uniform, his dark eyes staring out intensely from under that furrowed brow, the granite jaw set firm, he is the embodiment of the tough, noble British hero. *Zulu* has become one of those Bank Holiday traditions, wheeled out by television companies for every festive occasion; it is still guaranteed to attract healthy viewing figures more than forty years after it was first released. In a poll conducted by the British Film Institute, *Zulu* was ranked thirty-one in their list of the 100 favourite British films, while viewers of the satellite television channel Sky Premier voted it the eighth best film of all time, the second highest position achieved by a British film (only 1997's *The Full Monty* did better). As this book is being completed, the *Radio Times* has published a readers' poll of the greatest British films in which *Zulu* finished ninth overall and appeared at the top of the list of war films. The film has a peculiar place in the affections of the British public, keeping its star and producer in the public consciousness.

The film was the making of Stanley Baker, but it had its downside in that the film's popularity so overshadowed the rest of his career that his other achievements were rather forgotten. As a young film fan, my own initial knowledge of Baker's roles didn't extend much beyond *Zulu* and Joseph Losey's masterly *Accident* (1967). To a degree, Baker's decline from public recognition was a consequence of his own decision to work largely within British film and television. Unlike his young co-star in *Zulu*, Michael Caine, he never succumbed to the lure of Hollywood and so many of his finest films were small-scale British genre films which have unjustly faded from memory. When I came to research his career it was something of a revelation. I wrote an open letter to several of the newspapers covering south Wales where Baker had grown up, not knowing what response I might get. To my pleasant surprise, I had a large postbag of replies from people who had grown up with him or knew him at school in the mining village of Ferndale in the Rhondda valley. What particularly struck me was the pride of which the letters spoke, a genuine and unpretentious affection for a man who was clearly regarded as something of a hero, not just as a successful actor and film star but as someone who had never forgotten his roots, and had remained connected to the people he had come from. Baker had always expressed these feelings

1

publicly himself: in an interview he gave for *Photoplay* in 1969 he said: 'Acting can be an artificial business. That's why I go home whenever I can to the Rhondda valley. I do it to be with my own people. They live in a real way. It's a great leveller.'

Baker's journey took him a long way from his harsh upbringing during the depression of the 1930s. It was a progression that was both unusual in British cultural terms and yet indicative of a number of key changes which were to occur in British society, and cinema, during his lifetime. The story of how individuals from working-class backgrounds began to impact fundamentally on the cultural landscape of Britain from the 1950s onwards, particularly in the popular arts, has been well documented, and Baker is a characteristic example. Yet few of his generation had quite such a monumental climb towards the light. Growing up in a Welsh mining village with a disabled father who was unable to work following a mining accident was a situation from which few would have had the determination to escape. There was a general assumption during Baker's childhood that this wild, rough youngster would work in the mines along with his friends and his elder brother. Like his friend Richard Burton, it was an encounter with an inspirational teacher which changed his direction in life. Acting became his exit from the narrow world of the Rhondda, just as it might easily have been boxing, rugby or singing that provided the escape route. As a teenager he appeared in *Undercover* (1943) for Ealing Studios and acted with Richard Burton in the stage production of *The Druid's Rest* by Emlyn Williams. Success seemed to beckon, but the transition from promising juvenile to the world of adult stardom was not straightforward. An apprenticeship with Birmingham Rep followed, as well as an interruption for his National Service. As a struggling actor in the London of the early 1950s it was hard enough just to get walk-on roles, but then came *The Cruel Sea* (1953) and his film career was finally underway.

The transitions in his progress occurred rapidly as he established himself as a creditable villain in films such as *Knights of the Round Table* (1954) and *Helen of Troy* (1956), before becoming British cinema's favourite tough guy with *Hell Drivers* (1957) and *Hell is a City* (1960). By the early 1960s he was one of the most popular British stars as far as domestic audiences were concerned, as well as one of the highest paid. For film historian Andrew Spicer, his rise coincided with the development of youth culture in Britain, making Baker a perfect star for a new generation of discontented young people: 'an attractive, virile and ambitious hero, pursuing a combination of personal and social aspirations against a hostile environment'. These figures could be policemen or soldiers and sometimes, with the increasingly blurred moral boundaries of the 1960s, they were sympathetic criminals. As the decade progressed these roles continued, but he began to harbour new ambitions in two distinctly different areas. Working with expatriate American director Joseph Losey he began to exhibit a depth and complexity as an actor which had not previously been apparent, in art-house projects like *Eve* (1962) and *Accident*. He also found an interest in working behind the camera; *Zulu* was the first of several films he was to produce with his own companies, including the equally popular *The Italian Job* (1969). The actor had become a producer and executive, a player in the world of British cinema whose desire to come to the aid of a failing national film industry eventually led him into an abortive attempt to buy Shepperton Studios. The fallout from this was to damage his acting career, but ironically it was the small screen that came to his rescue. He had appeared on television from the early 1950s and been a key figure in founding HTV. At the end of his career it was on television that he achieved a kind of epiphany in the BBC version of *How Green Was My Valley* (1975).

These on-screen achievements are, obviously enough, reflections of the kind of man Stanley Baker was, but other parts of his career are equally illuminating in how they illustrate the typical lot of a jobbing actor. Baker was always at pains to play down the mystification of the film star, seeing it as job of work, albeit a well paid one, and acknowledging how fortunate he had been. As he told Clive James in a television interview for Granada's *Cinema* programme in 1972:

> I think acting, just acting, in someone else's movies for me is really like having a holiday. I enjoy acting very much and I suppose I can be described as indiscriminate when it comes to the choice of parts that I play in movies, because I like acting. I will act in anybody's movie if I think the part is right, you know, if I think I can add something to the part or the part can add something to my career – to what I want to do as an actor – and the money's right, then I'll do it. And it's good – I enjoy it. It's my life.

There is a touch of false modesty in this statement, and it's noticeable that he is referring only to acting, not producing, but it does convey the pragmatic view that he often took of his own career. An examination of his life in film is revealing in showing how that career was shaped by the wider British production context. Baker was a contract player with Alexander Korda and with the Rank Organisation in the 1950s. As such, he was often a chattel to be shunted into whichever acting slot needed to be filled at that moment. He was perfectly aware of the pecking order which kept him as a supporting player at Rank and was one of the first British stars to buy out his own contract and go freelance. His filmography reflects some of the dominant genres in British filmmaking with crime, action and war movies accounting for many titles. Changing audience tastes are apparent as films like *The Games* (1970) and *Perfect Friday* (1970) reflect the ambience of Swinging London, just as *The Cruel Sea* mirrored the attitudes of 1950s Britain. Baker was well aware of the degree to which the cinema is shaped by audiences; he told Clive James, 'In the final analysis what you do in the cinema comes from the public. If they like it, then it's good and successful.' His career also followed the changing economic patterns of British production with a fair share of 1960s European co-productions, American-backed costume epics, and low-budget caper films.

It was a career with many appealing dimensions to it. There was Baker the working-class hero. This was evident not just in the films, where he seemed to prefigure the emergence of a new generation of proletarian British stars like Michael Caine, Sean Connery and Albert Finney, but also in his private life where he strived to maintain his connection with the working-class culture which had formed him. Unlike Burton, Baker was regularly back in the Rhondda with *his people*; his commitment to local good causes never flagged. It was also apparent in his political beliefs; a lifelong socialist, he played an active part in supporting the Labour Party, particularly in their election campaigns in Wales. He was to speak movingly to Vincent Kane of BBC Wales in a television interview about how his upbringing in Ferndale, where poverty bred a fierce community spirit, instilled in him the roots of his socialist beliefs. If class was part of what he meant to audiences, then his Welshness was also crucial. In what was essentially an English national cinema he was inevitably an outsider, a quality which came through in many of his film roles and inadvertently added to his appeal to the young generation of the 1950s. It also maintained that sense of authenticity that was central to his appeal. Film historian Geoffrey Macnab sees Baker as a complimentary figure to Burton, 'two Welshmen who were truculent and self-destructive, not at all the types to do the publicists' bidding'. His abiding love of sport, gambling and the odd drink were also part of the mythology. The loyalty he felt to his family, both the one he was born into and the one he made with his wife Ellen, as well as the degree to which the land of his birth remained in his thoughts, were the stuff of reality, not myth.

These qualities were central to his contribution to British cinema, where he helped to break the stranglehold on stardom held by the English middle-class actors like Dirk Bogarde and Kenneth More. He became part of a cinematic revolution, connecting the films of the 1950s to the radicalism of the 1960s. In a national cinema which tended to favour nice, well-behaved chaps, he was awkward, explosive and refreshing. As Ellen Baker testifies, Americans liked him for this. This included directors like Losey and Cy Endfield, producers such as Joseph E. Levine, and the actors who became his friends, such as Robert Mitchum and Edward G. Robinson.

4

He had none of the affectations of class which Americans tended to read as British snobbery; he was a democrat, a 'working Joe' just like them. This tough guy persona has also helped to keep his screen persona relevant: the young Baker might just as easily have found employment as a hero or villain in the action genre of recent years. These aspects of his screen work, along with his class and nationality, are evidence of his considerable importance to the way British cinema developed in the 1960s and 1970s, as well as relating to ideas about the nature of masculinity in this period. He might well have been, as his friend Henry Cooper put it, 'a real man's man' but he was also able to suggest a vulnerability and complexity which made that masculinity more compelling and revealing.

Academic historians are often asked to justify their reasons for undertaking research and I can offer two in defence of this study of Stanley Baker's career. Baker has been an unjustly neglected figure in the recording of British film history, even overshadowed among Welsh stars by Richard Burton and Anthony Hopkins. When my own students ask who I am writing about and I offer up Stanley Baker's name, I am frequently greeted by blank faces. My response is to utter the magic word '*Zulu*', to which they invariably reply 'Oh, you mean the other guy – not Michael Caine.' I hope this book may go some way to explaining the not inconsiderable impact Baker had on the development of popular cinema in Britain. In researching this book, I sat through one or two films which might best be forgotten, but even in poor films the eye is often drawn towards to Baker. As his previous biographer Anthony Storey put it, 'he carried himself beautifully as if aware of how he wanted to look and well able to achieve his intentions.' His qualities as a star and actor deserve to be celebrated. As a consequence, this book is principally concerned with his working career and only draws on the more private aspects of his life insomuch as they affect that on-screen image. Secondly, on a more personal note, there is clearly something about Stanley Baker that many have found inspiring. In an age when it is commonplace to find fault with the stars of popular culture, Baker seems pretty close to the real thing: a screen hero. Perhaps the romantic instinct responds to his abiding love for his wife and children, or it's the sentimentalist who can't resist the image of Baker arriving back in Ferndale in his latest Rolls-Royce and filling up the seats with local children to give them a ride through the streets where he grew up. Nonetheless, there remains something moving in the notion that whatever success he achieved, he never forgot that it was those streets that made him.

CHAPTER ONE

Out of the Valleys

Driving up the Rhondda Fach through Tylorstown heading for Ferndale on a cold winter morning early in 2006, it is evident just how much this place has changed since Stanley Baker grew up here in the 1930s. And yet there is much that he might find familiar too. The valley is just as narrow, with the mountains looming up towards the sky, their tops disappearing in low cloud today. The neat terraces are still tightly packed in, snaking their way along the impossibly steep valley sides. There is still a sense of pride in the well-scrubbed doorsteps and brightly painted house fronts. One thing has definitely changed, however: the very reason that these villages grew up here in this wild setting is now gone. Baker could hardly fail to notice its absence as his family life, like that of almost everyone else living in Ferndale, revolved around it. The pits have gone. The village is certainly cleaner now. There are no slag heaps and no pithead dominating the landscape, but there are also no miners and Ferndale's main source of employment has vanished. This is a community left high and dry as the tide of a wave of industry has long since subsided. The economic hardships brought about by this change are evident in the number of 'For Sale' signs on those neat terraced houses, and in the occasional patches of wasteland and the odd derelict building. The signs of attempted regeneration are here too in the industrial estate and the vehicle components factory up the valley in Maerdy.

The house that Stanley Baker grew up in is still there at the bottom of Albany Street, a stone's throw from the rugby field. There is a heavy-looking plaque on the wall to commemorate the fact. Ellen Baker, married to Stanley for twenty-five years and his widow now for another thirty, delights in telling the tale of how the plaque came to be installed. Ferndale Council had paid for it and arranged a grand unveiling on what turned out to be a miserable, rainy day. Stanley and Ellen were the guests of honour, along with Stanley's good friend, the boxer Henry Cooper. The mayoress made a speech explaining how Richard Burton's plaque just a few valleys away at Pontrhydyfen had already been stolen no less than three times and how Ferndale Council had taken steps to ensure that this was not going to happen with Stanley's plaque. This had been achieved by having it embedded into the wall of the house. Anyone attempting to make off with it would have to take the house with them. Ellen remembers Stanley turning to her and remarking that as the house is also joined on either side to a lengthy terrace the thieves would have to take all the other houses in the street as well. Looking at this hefty memorial now it's easy to believe the story. Out near the rugby field where dogs are being walked is another memorial to Ferndale's most famous son. On a small pedestal is a second plaque, this one unveiled on 28 June 1996 to commemorate the twentieth anniversary of Baker's death. Lady Baker was also to attend this ceremony, but this time unaccompanied. Awarded by the Wales Cinema 100 Group as part of the celebrations for the hundredth birthday of cinema itself, this plaque looks at though it has seen rather better days. Its protective perspex screen is as scratched as an old film print and serves to obscure the memorial as much as it protects it.

Today I am being shown around Ferndale by Alwyn Davies and Alun Clement, who are going to help me get a feel for the place where Stanley Baker grew up. Alun is resident historian at Ferndale Rugby Club which is remembering Stanley's achievements by naming its new lounge after him. He is also writing a book about the history of Ferndale. Alwyn claims a distinctive Baker connection too, as part of the local choir which recorded 'Men of Harlech' for perhaps the most famous scene in Baker's most enduringly popular film, *Zulu*. They take me up to the top of Llanwono Mountain where Stanley played as a child and where his ashes were scattered on another day back in 1976. Alwyn recalls that occasion as being 'a three-ring circus' with ice cream vans and hot dog sellers making the most of the enormous crowd. It was also a day when Ferndale remembered its most famous son, the choir sang, and Harry Secombe arrived in his gold Rolls-Royce. Today the hilltop is full of discarded refuse, but nothing can diminish the extraordinary view from up here. The valley is laid out below, with the old site of the collieries clearly visible, along with the remains of the junior school Baker attended,but which burnt down some time ago. Suddenly the low clouds swirl along the valley and Ferndale disappears from view. It's easy to see why he chose this unique spot as his final resting place; even on a wet, windswept day like today it has an elemental power.

We drive over the hill to a quiet spot next to the Brynffynon pub. Here, in 1964, the forty members of the Ferndale Imperial Glee Singers spent two days working with the actor and singer Ivor Emmanuel and sound engineer Rusty Coppleman on the recording of 'Men of Harlech' for *Zulu*. The spot was chosen for its pristine quiet, but Alwyn remembers how the recording was interrupted by the unexpected sound of an airplane roaring overhead.

He also recalls warmly the generous catering laid on by Stanley who made sure that everyone was properly fed and watered. Rusty Coppleman had just come over from Spain where he was working with Charlton Heston and Sophia Loren on *El Cid*. Alwyn remembers asking what Coppleman made of Ferndale in comparison and was surprised to be told that in all his travels it was one of the best places he had ever been to, simply because he had never experienced such warmth and hospitality. Driving back into Ferndale we pass 'Box Canyon', as it is known locally, where the children of Ferndale would go camping, and still apparently do. Alun tells me that at night the lights of Ferndale when seen from the mountainside make the shape of a genie's lamp.

The Ferndale that Baker grew up in had already been the site of a quite remarkable transformation by the time he was born. In the first half of the nineteenth century the Rhondda valley was, as historian John Davies describes it, 'a pastoral paradise' largely unmarked by industrial development and thinly populated. It was the principal land owner in the Rhondda, the Marquess of Bute, who first opened up the seams of steam coal in which the area was so rich. Coal production in the Rhondda rocketed from 2.1 million tonnes in 1874 to 9.5 million in 1913, constituting a quarter of all the coal produced in Glamorgan. The railway had arrived in 1856 to take the coal down to the docks in Cardiff and from there around the globe. The pits meant jobs, and ones that were comparatively well paid for industrial workers. As a result, the economic development of the Rhondda was accompanied by a consequent population rise. John Davies describes an increase in the population of the area from less than a thousand in 1851 to an astonishing 167,000 by 1924, giving the Rhondda a greater population than the whole of Cardigan, Meirionnydd and Montgomery put together. The characteristic geography of the Rhondda prevented the building of large towns and instead led to the development of the long, straggling pit villages that trail up the valleys, and to the terraces of small cottages which allowed such a huge influx of people to be housed in such a small area. By 1911 there were 23,680 people crammed into each square mile of the Rhondda, giving it the highest density of population in the whole of England and Wales.

It's hard to overestimate the degree to which the coal industry dominated the life and culture of the Rhondda. In 1901 69 per cent of all men living there worked in mining. Gareth Elwyn Jones records that in 1913 there were 41,000 men and boys working in the coal mines of the Rhondda and that south Wales was then producing one third of the world's coal exports. It's no surprise then that when the industry started to go into decline the impact should be on a similar scale. The reasons for the reversal were varied and complex, but the decline came alarmingly quickly and the areas which produced steam coal were particularly badly hit. Changes in transport, where oil was rapidly taking the place of coal as the main source of fuel, exacerbated economic changes that affected the whole of south Wales. By 1929 coal production in south Wales had dropped to just 3 per cent of world output. In 1927, the year before Stanley Baker was born, unemployment in the once thriving village of Ferndale stood at 40 per cent. As John Davies puts it, the economy of the valleys was to suffer 'almost total collapse.' In that same year, 250 Rhondda men marched to London and unsuccessfully lobbied the government to respond to the valley's desperate plight; a survey had estimated that 2,500 children in the Rhondda were suffering from malnutrition.

Ferndale itself followed a similar trajectory. At the beginning of the nineteenth century it was a tiny farming community, but by the start of the next century its population was nearly 9,000, making it the largest town in the Rhondda Fach and the main centre for shopping. Today the population is a little more than half that figure. The 1901 census tells us that most houses in Ferndale were home to large families, some with more than ten children. The overwhelming majority at that time would have been Welsh speakers, although the Baker family were not. At the height of the mining industry there were five pits in Ferndale; all of them were closed by the 1960s, although the colliery at Maerdy remained open until 1990. The mines provided the major source of employment in Ferndale, with some jobs also on the railway or in the town's large number of shops and pubs. For all the comparative poverty that the people of Ferndale endured during the early years of the twentieth century, the village was also a bustling place full of social activity.

William Stanley Baker was born here, in the small terraced house at 30 Albany Street, on 28 February 1928. It was hardly an ideal time to be born, as Ferndale was already experiencing the economic depression that was spreading over the valleys. To make matters worse, Stanley's father had lost a leg in a mining accident in 1917 when he was just nineteen and consequently was largely unable to work from then on. The Ferndale collieries had been the site of a number of catastrophic mining disasters, including the loss of 178 men in 1867 and a further 53 two years later, both at Ferndale Number One. His father's accident was on a smaller scale, occurring when the ropes on the pit cage broke sending it plummeting down the shaft, but it was nonetheless a devastating blow to the family. Baker spoke movingly about the incident when he appeared in the BBC Wales documentary *Return to the Rhondda* in 1965. Stanley's birth seems to have been something of a surprise to the family, as his elder sister Muriel recounted to Anthony Storey. The Bakers already had two children, and there had been a third which had sadly died, when Mrs Baker found herself pregnant again: 'The last thing she wanted was Stanley coming along. And then, thinking about it, she hadn't got over losing my baby sister. But Stanley brought luck with him. Everything started to gradually get better once he was born.'

Stanley's father, John Henry Baker (known to everyone as Jack), had been born in 1898 and, like almost everyone else in Ferndale, had inevitably gone to work in the mine, until his accident brought this to an end. He married Elizabeth Louisa Lock on 1 April 1918. She was a year younger and, like him, had grown up in Ferndale of one Welsh parent and one English. The family quickly grew with the arrival of Frederick (Freddie) later that same year and then Muriel in 1920. Some years later Freddie would quiz his father on the fact that he had come into the world rather less than nine months after his parents had married. His father told him not to think of himself as 'illegitimate' but as a 'lovechild'. As Muriel recounted, he then added, 'If you ever find a woman you love as much as I love your mother, you'll be a very lucky man.' Stanley told Vincent Kane how his father had struggled to make enough money to support his young family, taking on various odd jobs, repairing boots, cutting hair and mending the miners' jacks (the tins they carried their food in). Occasionally he got short periods of work above ground at the pit.

Despite the difficulties of the family's situation, Jack Baker seems to have been a gentle, affectionate man, dedicated to his family. It's clear that Stanley adored his father and that he was an enormous influence on his own attitudes towards family life. He told Anthony Storey: 'He was a great man. I mean that. He really was. A great man. He was an atheist. He didn't believe in God. But he believed in people. And he loved children.' He went on to describe how his father would play football with him using his crutches as goal posts and how he taught Stanley to box. Muriel explained that Jack's atheism had arisen from the anguish he suffered at the early death of his own mother from cancer, but this didn't prevent him from being, in her words, 'the kindest man you ever could meet. All he could do was good for people.' The family were tight-knit and everyone played their part in helping to bring enough in to keep mouths fed. Muriel remembered how their mother would make toffee or small beer to sell. Stanley himself had odd jobs as soon as he was old enough and physically able to do them. At the age of eight or nine he was getting up (with his father's help) at 5.30 in the morning to do a milk round before school. Stanley's cousin John Wyatt, who was born in the same house as Stanley and grew up living with his parents in the house next door, recalls how hardworking the young Stanley was, doing two paper rounds to bring in a little money for the family. Despite these efforts, the family were still often dependent on charity. As soon as he was old enough, Freddie went out to work. Initially, his father tried his best to avoid him having to go down the pit and he was employed for a while in Samuel's Outfitters, but he hated it. That, and the peer pressure from other boys who were already working in the mine, took its toll and Freddie soon joined them underground. Muriel was then to go into service across the border in Bath. Barry Sullivan, who grew up just down the road from the Bakers at 32 Albany Street, remembers that despite the family's poverty Mrs Baker was a houseproud woman who always kept a 'tidy' home.

Stanley himself certainly doesn't seem to have viewed his childhood experiences as anything other than positive, even if he didn't wish the same on anyone else. When Vincent Kane suggested to him that his was a deprived childhood, his reply was emphatic:

> No, quite the contrary. Despite the fact that we didn't have a lot of food, I look back on my childhood as one full of the opposite to deprivation, full of advantages, because of my family basically and because of the people who surrounded us: an immensely strong communal feeling. People shared everything. People worked toward one end and that end at that time was, unfortunately, not to die of hunger. Everyone shared. If you didn't have something, someone else in the street or in the house next door gave it to you or lent it to you until you could pay them back.

These feelings about his upbringing are apparent in many aspects of his later life; not least in the socialism which was indelibly part of his make-up and in his determination to be a success in his career. Muriel told me: 'Stanley had an incredibly strong sense of purpose, even when he was young. He was absolutely positive he wasn't going to end up going down the mine. He was going to make sure that he got what he wanted out of life.' The legacy of his childhood was also there in the loyalty that he felt for his roots, to Ferndale and its people in particular.

And Ferndale has not forgotten him. On the chilly evening of 3 February 2006 I make my way to the warm welcome of Ferndale Rugby Club. Tonight is a special evening and the place is packed. Entertainment has been laid on in the form of a comedian/singer, a male voice choir, and part of the drum section of the Royal Welsh Regiment. They look splendid in their red tunics, a visual reminder of *Zulu*. The occasion that has brought all of this about is the opening of the Sir Stanley Baker lounge. Alun Clement has done a remarkable job decorating the lounge and the club's corridors with framed photographs from Stanley's films. There is a Zulu shield hanging above the bar, a signed poster for *Dingaka* (1965) on the wall and some fine portraits specially commissioned from a local painter. Stanley's name is inscribed on a display with his classmates from their primary school. In the corridor, guests come down past the collection admiring the photographs of a man who has been dead now for thirty years. What is remarkable is just how proud they remain of him and how connected they feel to this man who left Ferndale such a long time ago.

The beginning of that departure lies with a man named Glynne Morse. Stanley had been far from a model pupil at school. He moved up from the infants' school to Duffryn Juniors without making much of an academic impression. He remembered the latter with less than affection as a tin shack by the river which had been built by the pit owners and was known irreverently by its pupils as the Riverside Academy. Sport provided his only real area of success. He was good at swimming, football and boxing; anything that involved him in physical action, but, as he told Vincent Kane, he found sitting in a classroom trying to learn akin to torture. He also had something of a reputation as a tearaway, particularly when on the loose with his chief partner in crime, Billy Rossiter. The two boys were brought together by their shared poverty. He told Anthony Storey how the two families were the poorest of the poor, so that he and Billy even looked the same in their shabby clothes: 'We were like identical twins. And we both behaved in the same way. We both hated school and all it stood for.' Muriel recalled his rather fearsome reputation: 'The neighbours used to complain to our Dad about what Stanley did. You could say he was a menace. I was his sister, but I was frightened of him.' Howard Lloyd, who was at school with Stanley, told me how, when they attended Sunday school together, the Superintendent would always ask Stanley to sit at the front (the 'sedd fawr' in Welsh chapels) so that she could keep a close eye on him. Similarly, Ken Lewis (whose elder brother was in the same class as Stanley) remembers 'Spud' Baker, as he was known, as something of a bully and the Baker family as being particularly poor, even by Rhondda standards. All of this was to change with his move up to the secondary school in North Road and his meeting with its arts and crafts master, Glynne Morse.

Glynne Morse occupies a place in Stanley Baker's story that is not dissimilar to that taken by Philip Burton in the life of the young Richard Jenkins, soon to take his mentor's name and become the classical actor and Hollywood star Richard Burton. Morse was an amateur playwright who put on productions of his own work in the local working men's clubs and community halls, frequently giving parts to children from the school where he taught. He also ran a well-known amateur dramatic society, the Ferndale Arts Players. Baker often stated in interviews that it was Morse who had made him an actor, taking a rebellious boy and turning him into someone who had found a vocation in life. He told Vincent Kane that it was Morse who changed his attitude to school, so that he actually wanted to turn up in the mornings. This is a view shared by Ken Lewis of Ferndale who remembers taking part in amateur productions with Baker and says that Glynne Morse saw something in him which no one else had noticed. Muriel confirms that Morse saw the 'special' qualities which her brother possessed and was then able to inspire Stanley to believe in himself. Gareth Morse, Glynne's son, remembers how his father recognised in the young hooligan a 'physical vitality' which might be put to better use. He recalled how his father wrote a play, *The Light*, based on the life of Girolamo Savonarola, with Stanley cast in the lead role: 'He used to come to our house at 11 Wood Street two or three evenings a week, expected to know his lines, which he did. The play was put on in the church hall, Ferndale.'

Glynne Morse's own account of events gives more credit to the young Baker himself. He told the *South Wales Gazette* how he first spotted Stanley's talent in a school play:

> In spite of broad diction and playing, there was about him the spark of the theatre which properly nurtured might well kindle into a flame. So his time and energies were judiciously diverted into the grid of histrionics, harnessed as power to the making of a star instead of dissipated on tortuous escapades. Plays for boys suitable for full-scale production are scarce and faced with this dearth of material I wrote *The Haunted Chateau* expressly as a vehicle for giving Stanley his first real ground in stagecraft. His reading intensified, its range enlarged, there gradually emerged from Stanley a sense of rhythm and joy in the consonance and flow of words which was something quite unusual in a boy of his age.

Morse saw his role as encouraging and shaping a talent that already existed, but which lacked the proper means of expression. Baker's use of English may have left a good deal to be desired, but there was no mistaking the natural intelligence that lay waiting to be uncovered beneath the rough exterior. More than this, Morse recognised a determination and drive to succeed which he knew would be absolutely essential if Stanley was to fight his way from Ferndale to an unlikely career as a professional actor.

If the ability and the desire were already there waiting for Glynne Morse to ignite them, then their original source may well have been much closer to home. Hayden Jones, who went right through school with Baker, remembers that school play (he was in it too) and recalls the bravura of a young boy who relished the chance to swagger as a pirate chief. Muriel recalled the young boy who would come home from school and rehearse in front of a mirror to see what kind of effect he was having. Ellen Baker felt that both of Stanley's parents were the first inspiration for his gifts. His mother, who took part in three choirs, filled the house with singing and his father was constantly telling stories. His cousin Joan recollects the parties in the Baker household with her Aunty Liz and half the street invited in. Barry Sullivan also confirms that in his quiet way Baker's father was something of an entertainer, keeping the local children mesmerised with magic tricks and tall stories. During a period when he worked as a nightwatchman, groups of children would visit him to hear his stories. Muriel remembered how she, Freddie and the young Stanley would put on shows, using a table for a makeshift stage, with their father presiding over the performance. She also recalls Stanley dolled up in his best clothes reciting a poem in chapel: 'He was marvellous, you know, and everyone liked him. He was a star then you might say, and so confident, he was really like a little four-year-old professional.' For Stanley, however, there was never any question that it was Glynne Morse who opened the door for him to another life: 'Practically everything I am and certainly any success I've had as an actor I owe to Glynne. He taught me elocution, gave me books to read and all that sort of thing. And he wrote plays for me.' He never forgot the debt and when Glynne Morse retired from teaching Stanley bought him a house in Weston-super-Mare to make his home.

Baker's first real taste of the life that was to await him as an actor came in 1942 with the visit to Ferndale of the director Sergei Nolbandov. Nolbandov was in pre-production with a wartime propaganda film for Michael Balcon's Ealing production company. His film, *Undercover* (1943), was to tell the story of the partisans fighting against the Nazis in Yugoslavia. Nolbandov was scouting in Wales for locations to stand in for the mountainous landscapes of Yugoslavia. The film's narrative was set in a small village and centred on the school and its teacher, requiring a number of key supporting roles for children. A regionally based theatrical agent and talent scout, Joyce Marriott, had seen Baker in one of Glynne Morse's plays called *Liberation*, where he played a young Polish pianist, and suggested that Nolbandov come to see the end of term production that the thirteen-year-old Baker was starring in. As a result of this encounter, there was a further audition in Cardiff where, according to Glynne Morse, Baker saw off competition from 'all the best young actors in Wales, gold medallists and all'. Baker recalled to Clive James in their interview in 1972:

> Three or four days later I was taken to the Ealing Studios and did a screen test and I got the part. I know I was destined quite clearly and obviously to be, without any drama or nonsense, a coal miner – my brother was a coal miner, my father had been a coal miner, all the kids in my class ended up as coal miners. This was all there was in that place and suddenly I was an actor.

In a later press release for the Rank Organisation, Baker recalled how crucial Morse's role had been in proceedings: 'En route to London, in the train, he gave me last-minute coaching. I got the part, despite the fact that I came up against another juvenile actor, Richard Attenborough.'

He described to Clive James the excitement of going to London with the blitz raging and living in a hotel while the shooting of the film took place; the film's location work was undertaken near Brecon in south Wales. Glynne Morse managed to get permission from his education authority to accompany Stanley on his London adventure and was even offered a small role in the film. After each day's shooting at Ealing he would go back to his hotel where Morse would be waiting to rehearse the next day's scenes with him. The experience laid the seeds for the career that was to follow: 'After the film was finished, we went back to Ferndale. In the train, Glynne said to me: "Stanley, you're not going to be a miner. You're an actor!" and that was that! I really didn't have any say in the matter.' In reality, when the film was released in 1943, it was met with a fairly cool reception from critics. The trade paper *Kinematograph Weekly* suggested it was 'not particularly original, neither is it crystal clear, but it gets a move on and uses up plenty of ammunition'. Most recognised its obvious sincerity of purpose and a few acknowledged the power of some of its sequences to move the audience. However, its earnestness and tendency towards melodramatic clichés brought a fair amount of sarcasm from reviewers well used to the strategies of British propaganda films. Baker's role was relatively small and gets no specific mention in any of the reviews. Although Ealing's publicity materials drew attention to the film's south Wales locales and the use of Welsh schoolchildren in the cast, again Baker receives no specific mention. All of this is rather unfair as he has at least one scene of real distinction. When a Nazi officer interrogates the schoolboys, the young Baker is openly defiant. To teach him a lesson, he is then forced to watch the execution of several of his classmates. The sequence generates a good deal of emotion and Baker's reaction shots show genuine maturity. The firm jaw line is already recognisable, as is the intensity behind the eyes.

There were direct material benefits too from Stanley's early breakthrough. Muriel tells, with considerable feeling, the story of how Stanley returned from London with his wages, a quite substantial sum for a poor family, and in the manner of the miners he knew so well deposited the roll of notes into his mother's waiting lap. He had deliberately taken his pay cheque to a bank and changed his wages into single pound notes so as to have the maximum dramatic impact on his mother. However, once back in Ferndale things came back down to earth again with a bump. School was now finished and the fourteen-year-old Baker found himself working for the next six months as an electrician in a factory in Treforest. At least he wasn't down the mine, although unless things changed radically that remained a likely prospect. Then his second major stroke of good fortune occurred. An advert appeared in one of the local newspapers asking for Welsh youngsters to audition for the production of a new play by Emlyn Williams. It was to be called *The Druid's Rest*. The auditions were to be held at the New Theatre in Cardiff and so Glynne Morse again set about preparing his young charge. The casting director in charge of the auditions was Daphne Rye, who was given the task of finding a juvenile lead and an understudy for the role, along with a number of other youngsters for smaller roles. Daphne was later to become a good friend of Stanley's and had a home near to his in Spain. Baker went to the auditions accompanied by another of Glynne Morse's young hopefuls from Ferndale, Brynmor Thomas and a crowd of well-wishers from their home village. Among the supporting party was Tom Condon, who still lives in Ferndale. He remembers the excitement of the occasion and how Baker won the job of understudying the lead role. The lead role itself went to an actor three years older than Baker and from a village in a valley just a few miles away. It was the young Richard Burton.

The play was the first professional theatrical engagement for both young men. It began with a run of six months in the West End, which was then followed by a national tour. During the tour, in the spring of 1944, Burton was called up for his National Service and Baker took over the lead role. As Glynne Morse recalled to Anthony Storey, 'He came back from that with a lot of experience and not all of it of the stage by a long way.' Baker lived in digs in London with Burton and the two Welsh teenagers, a long way from home, were determined to enjoy every moment. They were both earning money and, as Baker told Vincent Kane, they had 'a hell of a time'. Burton later claimed that when the play opened in Liverpool Stanley had arranged for some female company and contrived to introduce him to sex. Considering the age gap between the two it seems more likely that it was the other way around, a view which Ellen Baker shares. In his affectionate biography of Burton, Melvyn Bragg describes the antics of the two boys as they drank, fought, chased after girls, smashed the windows in dressing rooms and took potshots with their peashooters at the half-naked chorus girls sunning themselves on the roof of an adjacent building. Ellen recalls her husband telling her that the matron assigned to look after the welfare of the two boys resigned from her post unable to cope. It was the beginning of a loyal friendship between the two that was to have its ups and downs, but which lasted throughout Baker's lifetime. The experience in London was also a tantalising glimpse of a possible, different life to come, one which he was increasingly determined to grasp hold of.

The first step to realising that ambition was to obtain a proper professional training. Baker recounted in a Rank press release in the late 1950s how Glynne Morse hatched the plan:

> Glynne said to me: 'What you need, my lad, is two years in repertory.'

> 'Fine' I said, 'but how?'

> 'Leave it to me' he said and he wrote straight off to the late Sir Barry Jackson of the Birmingham Repertory Theatre. I afterwards heard that Sir Barry had never met Glynne and, anyway, the Birmingham Rep. was full up at the time, but he had been so impressed by the letter that he gave me an audition.

> And I got taken on . . . two glorious years of acting parts from the classics in one of the finest reps in the world.

Morse was again the architect of his success, preparing him for the audition with lines chosen from one of the plays he had written specially for Stanley. According to Morse's version of events, it only took a few lines for Sir Barry to be sufficiently impressed to provide Stanley with the immediate offer of a place. He now found himself in exulted company. Among his fellow actors at Birmingham Rep, a company which could boast Laurence Olivier in its alumni, were Paul Schofield, Paul Eddington and Dennis Quilley, with whom he shared a flat. Quilley later recalled a young boy who seemed much older than his years and who knew how to look after himself. Baker viewed his years with the company as a long overdue literary education. He later described how the company would produce twelve plays in twelve months, with one month for rehearsal and one month of performance. There were productions of Shakespeare, Chekhov and Ibsen for the young actor to cut his teeth on. Among his roles was that of Hector Malone in a production of Shaw's *Man and Superman* during 1945, directed by the young Peter Brook. The result of all this experience was not just an intensive training as an actor, but a kind of cultural awakening as Baker discovered a new world of literature and art that had not been open to him before. He now considered himself to be a professional actor for the first time.

This idyll was brought to an end in 1946 in the same manner as Richard Burton's run in *The Druid's Rest* had been, by the call of National Service. Two and a half years in the Royal Army Service Corps was a substantial interruption to the burgeoning acting career, even if he did end up reaching the rank of sergeant. Glynne Morse stayed in touch and did his best to keep Baker's education going by sending him books to read. Baker would be required to write back with a report on his reading and Morse would then correct his English. These were years spent marking time and waiting to resume his life as an actor. His old school friend Hayden Jones unexpectedly encountered Baker again during National Service when they were both on a course at an army base in Cirencester. Baker was now stationed in London but spent every weekend during the course going back home to Ferndale. Hayden travelled with him and remembers a young man who was very pleased to be escaping back to some home comforts.

Returning to civilian life in 1948 was a considerable shock to the system. He was no longer a child protégé, just a jobbing young actor who needed to start his career all over again. The breaks were slow in coming and he was often forced back on mundane jobs, working as a waiter and washing dishes in a Knightsbridge restaurant, selling socks in a department store. There were small roles in the theatre, including a spell with Middlesex Rep for whom he took the lead in productions of *Treasure Island* and *Wuthering Heights*, as well as a part in the West End run of a new Terence Rattigan play, *Adventure Story*, with Paul Schofield. There was also a series of walk-ons in a number of long forgotten, low-budget films. He was a reporter in *Whispering Smith Hits London* (1951), a milkman in *Cloudburst* (1951), and a policeman who is called to give evidence in *Your Witness* (1950). Of nine fleeting appearances in three years the most substantial film he appeared in was *Captain Horatio Hornblower R.N.* (1951), a Technicolor seafaring saga adapted from C. S. Forester's novels, made in Britain by Warner–First National and starring Gregory Peck. He played the bosun, but even here his role is relatively insignificant; his name doesn't appear in the opening credits and he is billed eleventh in the end credits, just above another future star, Christopher Lee. There is no mistaking the handsome face of the youthful Baker, but the part requires him to do little more than dash about shouting instructions at other sailors. Along with many other young actors of the period, he quickly discovered that there were better openings in the shiny new world of television. For the small screen he appeared in *Choir Practice*, taking a role which Ivor Novello had previously played in the radio version of the play, as well as portraying Petruchio in Shakespeare's *The Taming of the Shrew*. One positive note in these years was the rekindling of his friendship with Richard Burton. They found digs together in Streatham in South London and quickly set about enjoying themselves again. As Burton's biographer Penny Junor put it, such was their success at picking up girls at the local dance hall that 'they were known as the Palais de Danse Kings of Streatham'.

Finally, his patience and application were rewarded with a real opportunity when in 1950 he appeared in the stage production of Christopher Fry's *A Sleep of Prisoners*. Baker was considered for the part thanks to the help of his friend, the actress Diana Graves. She knew Christopher Fry and persuaded him to take a look at the young Baker. Baker later recalled to Anthony Storey how 'the very next day I went to Fry's house and I read for him and I got the part, I got it on that day and my agent couldn't get me anything. That really changed things for me. It was a four-character play and a very good part and it was very, very successful.' The play centred around four soldiers who have been captured during an unspecified war. While in transit they are held prisoner overnight in a church and each of them has a dream. The play moves backwards and forwards between the reality of their situation and their dreams which combine violent recollections of war with biblical references. Its themes were strongly anti-war and reflected the pacifism of Fry who was a Quaker. Alongside Baker, the play featured Leonard White, Denholm Elliott and Hugh Pryse, and all the members of the cast received strong notices. At one midnight matinee the audience included Laurence Olivier and Vivien Leigh, Orson Welles, Ralph Richardson and John Gielgud. To add to the atmosphere of the staging it was performed in churches. For the London production, the church used had been damaged in the blitz and part of the section behind the altar had been completely blown out, providing for an even more telling mood. The play toured successfully in Britain and then took its cast to the United States for a New York run and a national tour. Christopher Fry accompanied the production on its travels and seems to have taken a particular shine to its youngest actor (Baker was still only twenty-two), forming a friendship with him. He later became godfather to Stanley's eldest son, Martin.

This wasn't the only major event to take place during this year. Around this time the young (but already established) actress Ellen Martin was appearing in a production of the play *Treasure Hunt* at the Apollo Theatre in London's West End. Rationing was still taking its toll on everyday life, so she and a fellow actress decided to organise a get-together with their friends to make omelettes for lunch. Entry to their backstage rooms was dependent on bringing along some eggs or other ingredients. The young Richard Burton, who was appearing in a play in the theatre nearby, arrived with a friend who was carrying a bag of cherries, but no eggs! Ellen was immediately attracted to one of the young men and her friend assumed she must be talking about the charismatic Burton. However, as she recalls, it wasn't Burton but 'the tall, beautiful one' who had taken her eye. The friend informed her that his name was Stanley Baker and warned her that if she pursued him she was likely to become another one of 'Baker's dozen', such was his reputation, but she concedes that it was a fate that she was quite happy to accept. That night she went to a party with her then boyfriend and Baker was there again. They were almost immediately inseparable and the boyfriend was forgotten. Within a week of first meeting they were engaged and on 22 October 1950 at St George's Church in Hanover Square, London, they were married.

Ellen came from a comfortable middle-class background, but found herself readily taken into the Baker clan. Her own father was at first resistant to his daughter's infatuation but an ultimatum from Ellen soon put a stop to that and he ended up buying the young couple their first home together. Ellen, who had trained at RADA at the same time as Roger Moore, first saw her husband act in *A Sleep of Prisoners* and vividly recalled the occasion to Anthony Storey:

> The whole evening was Stanley. He was superb, thrilling. It was the same, exactly the same thrill at that time as when Richard (Burton) walked on the stage and you were very aware that here was a strong presence and a wonderful, a marvellous voice and in those first minutes, first seconds, there was a tremendous impact. Stanley had such authority and such maturity too.

Above all, she was struck by the same thing she had noticed that first day she saw him in the West End; it was the way he moved, with a grace and rhythm which belied his physical strength and stature. It was a quality which would attract the eye of filmgoers when his screen career eventually took off.

The other major event of 1950 was at the very opposite end of the emotional spectrum for Baker. His father, who he worshipped, became seriously ill and quickly declined, dying at the age of just fifty-two. Ellen was never to meet him as her trip to see Stanley's family in Ferndale was postponed due to his father's condition. Stanley was afraid himself that his father might be gone before he could get to see him as he had to honour a contract to play a small role in a television play, but he did manage to see him one final time. He later recalled with some bitterness that he was so poor at that time that he had to borrow the £5 needed to pay for his father's funeral arrangements. Ellen finally met the family about one month after the funeral; they were married the following week. It was one of the great regrets of Stanley's life that his father was never to see his success, although he did at least witness the beginnings of what was to come. Years later, when speaking to the press on the twentieth anniversary of her brother's death, Muriel recalled an odd coincidence. Both she and Stanley had had very similar dreams about their father around the same time in the early 1970s. What had particularly struck her was that Stanley interpreted this as some kind of premonition that he too would have an early death. She described to me how in her dream their father had called out to her but she was unable to reach him, whereas in Stanley's dream he was able to be with his father and it was this that he read as some kind of omen.

Stanley's new wife was to have an immediate impact on the development of his career. In 1951 Ealing Studios were in the early planning stages of a film version of Nicholas Monsarrat's popular Second World War naval story *The Cruel Sea* (1953). Ellen had been approached to play the part of a Wren, a role eventually given to the then unknown Virginia McKenna, but had already made a decision to end her acting career to support her husband and to have children. Ironically, having made this decision she then found herself bombarded with offers of work in the theatre. While in America with *A Sleep of Prisoners*, she had given the book to Stanley to read and they agreed that he would be perfect for the key supporting role of First Lieutenant Bennett. On their return to England, she contacted the film's director Charles Frend to ask him to consider her virtually unheard of husband for the part. Baker told Clive James how he had written from America to Frend asking if he could test for the part. When he heard from his agent that the part had already been cast (with another actor represented by the same agent), Baker persisted in approaching the director and was rewarded with the chance of a little work taking part in a 'stooge test'. The test would involve Baker feeding lines to another actor who was being screen-tested, in this case Donald Sinden who was being considered for the part of another of the officers, Lockhart. Baker was to earn £5 for his trouble. He recalled:

> Suddenly in the middle of the test – I know it sounds romantic and untrue but it isn't, believe me it's true – Charlie Frend said 'OK, we've got that, let's turn the camera around' and the moment he turned the camera around on me I knew he'd give me the part in spite of the fact that they'd already cast an actor in the part. They saw the rushes the next day. At the end of the day Charlie Frend called me and said 'Are you free?' and I said 'No, I've got a lot of things to do at the moment – of course I'm free' and I got the part.

Baker couldn't recall the name of the poor actor who had been promised the part but remembered that he was paid off to let Baker to take the role. The anecdote says a great deal about the level of determination and drive which the young Baker possessed.

It was nine years now since his first film appearance as a boy in *Undercover*, plucked from Glynne Morse's end of term show and carried off to Ealing, where he was now to appear as supporting player in their most prestigious production of the year. He was a married man and at the start of his mature career in films. In some ways he was already a long way from Ferndale and the terrace in Albany Street, but in another, deeper sense he was not. He continued to visit home on a regular basis. Ken Lewis, Stanley's cousin, remembers him coming back to Ferndale and dropping in on his parents who would give Stanley a parcel of homemade food to take back to London with him. In exchange he would give his Uncle Bill a ten shilling note, which in those days of hardship in the Rhondda was a more than generous gesture. Ferndale had instilled in him a will and inner strength without which he could never have come the distance he already had. It had also given him a set of values, a belief in community and family, which he carried with him.

CHAPTER TWO

The Man you Love to Hate

There was no doubt as far as Stanley Baker was concerned as to just how important *The Cruel Sea* was to his career, and this despite the fact that the role of Bennett was by no means the lead. If anything, his character is the villain of the piece. He explained to Vincent Kane, 'It wasn't the star part, but it was the best part, the flashiest part.' He also acknowledged that it was the easiest part, if only in the sense that, despite appearing for merely the first twenty minutes of the film and in barely half a dozen scenes, the part of Bennett was virtually guaranteed to make a sizeable impact on audiences. When Vincent Kane puts it to him that this was his lucky break, there is an unmistakable glint of determination in his eye as Baker replies that luck is not enough on its own; he was ready to take full advantage of his chance when it came, he argues. Pragmatically, he also knew that being unknown had increased his chances of getting this small role as he was relatively cheap to employ.

The Cruel Sea belongs to a group of British films made during the 1950s and early 1960s which recall the events of ten or twenty years earlier when Britain was in the midst of war. Many of them portray events from the Second World War with more than a hint of nostalgia, harking back to Britain's 'finest hour' to commemorate individual heroism and the community spirit of the 'people's war' in such a manner that even tragic events tend to be seen through rose-tinted spectacles. Films in this cycle include *633 Squadron* (1964), *Carve Her Name with Pride* (1958), *Reach for the Sky* (1956) and *The Dam Busters* (1954). Film historian James Chapman has suggested that these films recreated what seemed, from the perspective of the 1950s, a time of moral certainties when Britain was sure of its place in the world, offering a 1950s audience something innately comforting, if conservative. In retrospect, *The Cruel Sea* doesn't entirely conform to the usual pattern of these films. It is certainly made in Ealing's established house style, with the emphasis on low-key realism, seen here in the meticulous build up of detail depicting life on board the *Compass Rose* and in the dovetailing of documentary footage into the fictional narrative. What is strikingly different is the nearly relentless emphasis on the horrors of war, most memorably depicted in the sequence where the ship's commander, Ericson (Jack Hawkins), is forced to kill British sailors who are stranded in the water directly over the U-boat that he is pursuing.

More characteristic is the focus on male friendship and camaraderie. In a key scene, Donald Sinden's Lockhart tells his fiancée (Virginia McKenna) that his friendship with Ericson is the only positive thing that he can think of in his wartime experiences. Christine Geraghty has suggested that British war films of this period tend to emphasise the importance of male groups and bonding, so that entering into a relationship with a woman is 'to open oneself up to fears about her safety or her faithfulness and such fears are incomparable with the masculine task of fighting the war efficiently'. In *The Cruel Sea*, Sinden's character is offered the chance of his own command but would rather remain at the side of Ericson. This is certainly a world of stiff upper lips, dominated by highly traditional notions of what it means to be male. As Geraghty suggests, 'unable to admit to feeling, the heroes of the war films can scarcely articulate emotion, let alone act on it, and what pleasure they have seems to come from their skill with and control over machines'. Again, *The Cruel Sea* doesn't entirely fit with this analysis as one of its most powerful scenes is of Ericson's breakdown after the death of the sailors when he is seen with tears running down his face, even if this has only been released with the help of several gins. What is also noticeable about this particular group of men is just how overwhelmingly middle-class they are. It may be a problem of seeing the film fifty years after it was made, but even audiences of the time must have been struck by the gentlemanly tones and clubbable manner of Denholm Elliott, Donald Sinden and John Stratton as Ericson's officers, although this is undeniably a feature of many British films of the period. It's in this context that Baker's appearance in the film is so startling. As Andrew Spicer describes it, 'when he returns, drunk, from his shore leave, he is shown framed in the doorway, the gross outsider, as seen from the point-of-view of the sober middle-class group'.

We first encounter Baker as he makes his way across deck, striding towards the camera. The lighting is low, but not as dark as the scowl across his face. He looks tough and intimidating, his eyes hard as he barks: 'I'm the First Lieutenant around here and don't you forget it.' He immediately catches sight of the callow faces of the two new officers, played by Sinden and Stratton, and interrogates them on their knowledge of the ship. The key to his character is quickly revealed, however, when Sinden confidently answers his inquiry as to how many fire points there are on board. Stratton is amazed that Sinden's character knew the answer, but in fact he didn't. He just guessed that the First Lieutenant didn't know either and therefore couldn't contradict his answer. Bennett is revealed to be a phoney and a bully. When Denholm Elliott joins the crew it is quickly evident that the three young officers have an affinity that they don't share with Baker's character. Much of this is based on class. In their civilian lives they were previously a journalist, a barrister and a bank employee, occupations differentiated from Bennett who was a used car salesman. He reveals his lack of class credentials in other ways too: he gets drunk and is the only crew member who seems to enjoy the nasty sausages the chef serves for dinner. Ellen Baker told me that Stanley actually shot a scene with Megs Jenkins (another fine Welsh actor) in which his roughness is made so apparent that the censor objected; she and Stanley were shown the initial version by the film's director and producer. Nonetheless, Baker's judgement about the potential of his role is proved right. Although Bennett is a thug and a fraud, escaping active duty by faking an ulcer (a course of action that is actually subtly suggested to him by the other three, so that they can get rid of him), he is still a more compelling figure than his fellow recruits. It is their cut glass accents and glib manners that have dated, whereas Baker's pushy, swaggering Bennett still seems fresh and dynamic. Within twenty minutes he is out of the film, but not out of the memory.

The film proved to be a major critical and commercial success in Britain. Other than the odd disparaging comparison with the original novel, the press reception was full of praise. Jack Hawkins was singled out in particular, with reviewers regarding it as his finest performance to date, but both Donald Sinden and Denholm Elliot were also well received. Stanley fared less well, with few critics paying him much attention. However Leonard Mosley writing in the *Daily Express* was more prescient: 'At the beginning of the film there is a performance from a newcomer named Stanley Baker, playing the part of a braggart and a bully – and he looks so genuine that you hate him from the moment you first notice his sneer and hear the nasty rasp of his voice.' The film received a BAFTA nomination as Best Film and one for Hawkins as Best Actor, as well as an Oscar nomination for Eric Ambler's adaptation. A more surprising plaudit was the award of a Selznick Golden Laurel for encouraging 'mutual understanding and good will between the peoples of the world.' Ealing made little use of Baker in their publicity campaign. Despite fifth billing, his name does not appear on the main poster used and his image is not among those released for the central promotion of the film. In press books released by Ealing his name appears a long way down and he is referred to only as an 'athletic Welshman' and the son of a miner. Nonetheless, he had acquitted himself well in what was one of the key British films of its year. His success was never in doubt for at least one fan; his mother. The film was shown at a special screening in Ferndale and at Stanley's first on-screen appearance Mrs

Baker apparently leapt from her seat to inform the audience 'that's my son'. They suggested that she take her seat again but nothing could stop her from crying when he is invalided off the ship.

One immediate consequence of Baker's appearance in *The Cruel Sea* was that he now found himself in regular employment in films, a situation which was to continue for the rest of his career. He initially found himself working for Warwick Films, a company recently founded by two American producers, Irving Allen and Albert 'Cubby' Broccoli: the latter was to gain fame for bringing James Bond to the big screen. They had relocated to Britain as it offered lower production costs than Hollywood, as well as the chance to obtain funding via the Eady Levy (a tax on cinema admissions used to boost British production). Their films were to be low-budget but would strive to give the impression of having Hollywood production values. They were also aimed squarely at an international market, something which was not always the case with British films of the period. A distribution deal with Columbia gave them access to world markets. This strategy was apparent in their first outing, and Baker's debut with them, *The Red Beret* (1953), released in the United States as *Paratrooper*. Although put together on a tight schedule, the film was still shot in Technicolor and puts much of its emphasis on battle scenes. To appeal to international audiences the American star Alan Ladd takes the lead and the British actors are deployed in supporting roles. The film was co-scripted by Richard Maibaum and directed by Terence Young, both of whom would also be central in bringing James Bond to the cinema.

Seen now, the film is a fairly routine wartime action-adventure yarn based loosely on real events and characters. It tells the story of the Parachute Brigade, including the raid on the German radar station at Bruneval. Historical fact is thinly disguised, so that the real life Major John Frost who led the attack has become Major Snow (Leo Genn) and the radar specialist, Sergeant Cox, has been renamed as Sergeant Box. Reality is manipulated to allow Ladd to appear as a guilt-stricken volunteer known as 'Canada' who steps into the breech when his commanding officer is wounded. War movie clichés abound and the dialogue sequences separating the action are mainly turgid. The film gave Harry Andrews his first film role (he was to appear in a remarkable number of films with Baker during the 1950s), but for Stanley the experience was something of a mixed blessing. Apart from playing a relatively minor role, and being well down the billing, the producers seem to have decided that his accent was too difficult for American audiences and he was dubbed over. Baker had already suffered the fate of many other Welsh actors, Burton included, in having spent some years trying to smooth the Welsh inflections out of his voice to make him acceptable for the English stage and an English dominated film industry based in London. Apparently this was not enough for *The Red Beret* and so he was robbed of one of his most distinguishing trademarks. Ironically, the film also features another Welsh actor, Donald Houston (whose brother Glyn had been in *The Cruel Sea*), playing a Welsh character inevitably called 'Taffy', but he was deemed sufficiently understandable to escape dubbing.

One positive thing to come from the film was the friendship which Baker struck up with Alan Ladd. It was the first of a number of such friendships he was to forge with American actors, including Edward G. Robinson and Robert Mitchum. Ellen Baker suggests that they found in Stanley none of the snobbery or affectedness which they sometimes encountered with British actors. To them he seemed as classless as any American archetype. Baker was to appear with Ladd again in the second of Warwick's British-based action films, *Hell Below Zero* (1954), rather vaguely adapted from a Hammond Innes novel and helmed by the accomplished American director Mark Robson. The film is set largely in the Antarctic and features Joan Tetzel as Judie Nordhal whose father, the captain of a whaling fleet, has seemingly committed suicide. Ladd is the American adventurer, Duncan Craig, who joins up with her as she heads south to find the truth about her father's death. Baker plays Erik Bland, the villainous son of her father's business partner who, of course, has actually murdered the unfortunate captain. To add a little extra spice, Erik is also Judie's former lover. For Baker the film meant an extraordinary fourteen week trip to the Antarctic for the location shooting. As he told Clive James, 'I would have paid if I'd had the money, but they were paying me and that was just an incredible thing.'

The film has the typical merits and deficiencies of Warwick's output. Little effort was put into the dialogue and the actors are given flatly drawn characters to play. The cheap sets used for interiors and close-ups contrast badly with the exteriors shot on location which are striking and make full use of Technicolor. The semi-documentary scenes depicting the everyday business of a whaling fleet, with much bloody hacking about of the whales, are liable to horrify the sensibilities of many modern viewers but undeniably provide a remarkable visual record of the industry. Baker again catches the eye in another dastardly supporting role, although we have to wait until nearly halfway through the film for him to make his first appearance. The script gives him precious little to work with, but he is allowed a couple of glowering close-ups to establish an appropriate sense of menace. As is so often the case with villains, he at least proves more memorable than the two leads, with Ladd rather bland as the hero and far from believable in his action scenes. Similarly, there is little romantic spark between Ladd and

Joan Tetzel. Baker eventually receives his inevitable comeuppance after an ice pick fight with Ladd on some decidedly unconvincing studio-made ice floes.

Ladd was to make another feature with Warwick, the inadvertently humorous Arthurian fantasy *The Black Knight* (1954), although this time without Baker. Their friendship was further cemented when several of Baker's friends from south Wales were used, at his behest, on the film as extras or on stunt work. Part of the film's location work was carried out at the picturesque folly Castell Coch, not far from Cardiff. Baker took the opportunity to give his new American friend a tour of his home town of Ferndale. What Ladd made of Ferndale or Ferndale made of him is unrecorded. Between these projects for Warwick, Baker appeared in a twenty-minute short film, *The Tell-Tale Heart* (1953), adapted from the macabre story by Edgar Allan Poe, with Baker taking the part of the author, and then the more substantial *Knights of the Round Tale* (1954). The film was made by the American giant MGM at their British studios at Elstree, with extensive location work in Ireland and Devon. It was an expensive retelling of the Arthurian legends, shot in the new cinematic marvel of Cinemascope (making it the first use of a widescreen process in a British film). Baker was not the initial choice for the film's chief villain, Mordred, but stepped in to replace George Sanders after he had fallen out with the producers. As reported by the *Sunday Chronicle*, this was a considerable break for the man who had played the 'boor and braggart' Bennett in *The Cruel Sea*; they suggested that he was making a name for himself – 'as a bully'. Baker seems to have made the most of the opportunity: 'I enjoyed doing it – riding horses and wearing costume and bathing in the grand manner. It was like Hollywood set in Devon – it was very funny, a great experience and very enjoyable.'

Baker was given fifth billing on the film behind its American stars, Robert Taylor (Lancelot), Ava Gardner (Guinevere), Mel Ferrer (Arthur), and Anne Crawford (Morgan le Fey). Again, MGM's publicity campaign made little use of Baker and in most of the posters the typeface for his name is noticeably small in comparison with the Hollywood names who were expected to ensure its box office appeal with American audiences. The film was released for Christmas in the United States and did reasonable business, but it was poorly received by the British press who felt that it took itself far too seriously. However, Baker was singled out for praise by a number of the critics, with the reviewer for the *Sunday Graphic* admiring 'the fiery villainy of Stanley Baker' and the *Sunday Express* describing him as 'properly murderous.' Seen now, the film certainly suffers from slow pacing and a ponderous approach, as well as from the unfortunate decision to use a form of cod Shakespearian language and delivery for the dialogue. This results in such tortuous gems as 'ride alone you shall not' and 'she ever grows more beautiful'. The film's chief appeal is visual: the cinematography by David Lean's future collaborator and multiple Oscar-winner Frederick A. Young and his assistant Stephen Dade (who would later photograph *Zulu*) makes sumptuous use of colour (the film was shot in Eastmancolor, but printed in Technicolor) and of the Irish landscape. The set designs by Alfred Junge, who had done such wonderful work on Michael Powell and Emeric Pressburger's *Black Narcissus* (1947), are certainly fine and were recognised with an Oscar nomination. The battle scenes teem with extras, although some of the stunt work is inferior. Baker is striking in his scenes, first appearing suitably clad in black and establishing himself as the villain by having one of Arthur's men thrown from a cliff into a muddy bog. Mercifully, he is allowed to speak in his own voice and delivers his lines with a real sense of conviction and theatrical panache, something lacking in Robert Taylor's flat delivery.

In these films Baker had begun to establish a recognisable screen persona as British cinema's favourite bad man of the moment. Sheldon Hall suggests that this typecasting was 'dictated by his brusque, surly manner, deep-set brown eyes, stony brow and strong jaw'. The press began to latch on to this image and build stories around it. For the London *Evening Standard* he was 'the face Britons hate', although they quoted Baker as complaining 'even an actor with a face like mine sighs for an audience's love sometimes'. Readers were informed by *The Star* that 'you will love hating Mr Baker'. They went on to suggest that 'in Stanley Baker British filmmakers have found a young man capable of bringing back the great days of screen villainy' and compared him favourably with Hollywood villains of the silent era like Erich von Stroheim. In an interview with the *Evening Standard*, Baker seemed sanguine enough about these developments: 'I should worry. The money's good. And, furthermore, I have a wife, twins, a large house in Wimbledon and a Jaguar to support. Besides I haven't got the face to be a glamour boy. Look at it closely, describe what you see.' The accompanying photograph shows a suitably intense, glowering figure. Later in the same piece Ellen corrects this impression, suggesting that 'actually he's a pet. A devoted father and an obedient husband. The face? I think it's charming.' Looking back now, Ellen agrees that he took a pragmatic view of the typecasting that was beginning to occur. For Stanley, these films were enjoyable to make (often involving an expenses-paid trip to a pleasant location), he was becoming better known to audiences and, in any case, it was a great deal better to be an employed actor than the unemployed one he had been just a few short years before. And there was the new house in Wimbledon, as well as a growing taste for expensive cars and for gambling.

More importantly, on 8 March 1953 the family had been expanded by the addition of the twins, Martin and Sally.

Baker was blunt in explaining to Clive James his attitude to these roles:

> I'd heard and read a lot of this stuff of actors being typecast and things like that, that it was an awful thing. All I knew it was a chance to act, a chance to earn money, a chance to gain experience – so I wanted to do it. And I don't care what the part would have been at that stage in my career. I would have done anything, you know.

When Vincent Kane asked him about his typecasting as a villain, he smiled broadly and explained that for him it was simply a means to gain experience as an actor while being paid well for it. He knew even then that a point would arrive when these roles would no longer be enough for him, but for the moment they were serving their purpose. And so the villainy continued in a spate of expensive costume films. *Helen of Troy* (1956) was shot during the latter part of 1954 and early 1955 on location in Italy. It was again produced by an American company, this time Warner Brothers, who were taking advantage of favourable exchange rates and the locations which Europe could offer them. Hollywood was already beginning to feel the impact of changes in the leisure habits of audiences at home. The arrival of television was spreading alarm among normally steely studio executives who, for the first time in cinema's short history, could see that this was a genuine challenge to their monopoly on providing the public with visual entertainment. As a result, they poured money into ensuring that the cinema could provide attractions which television could not compete with. If the television image was small, the cinema screen would get even bigger (or wider, at least) and if television was monochrome then films would be in glorious colour. What better vehicle to show off these spectacular attractions than an historical epic, hence the proliferation of such films in the 1950s and early 1960s. *Helen of Troy* was to be presented in Warnercolor and Cinemascope and, according to its publicity, cost a then unheard of $6 million and featured a staggering cast of 30,000 extras.

The Baker family found themselves ensconced in sunny Rome for the duration of the five-month shoot. If this wasn't sufficient incentive, Baker was to be paid the not inconsiderable sum of £30,000 for his services. It's not difficult to see why such offers proved hard to resist. Ellen Baker recalls the holiday atmosphere of that time and the pleasure of escaping from a damp, dreary Britain. At one point, a mix-up in the shooting of the film's elaborate battle sequences resulted in a delay of several weeks. To keep the cast happy they were shipped to Capri while they waited for work to begin again. Weekly expenses of £300 per person continued to be paid during this enforced vacation and Ellen remembers the money arriving each week by boat! There were other pleasant distractions back in Rome, including the starlets and models who would hang around in hope of catching someone's eye. Among them Ellen remembers a very young and beautiful Ursula Andress who would later star opposite Baker in *Perfect Friday* (1970).

Helen of Troy featured two relative unknowns, Jack Sernas and Rossana Podesta, in the lead roles of Paris and Helen, but their relative inexperience and lack of box office appeal was to be offset by a roster of notable British character actors in supporting roles. Alongside Baker as Achilles were Sir Cedric Hardwicke as Priam, Niall MacGinnis as Menelaus, and Harry Andrews as Hector. A youthful Brigitte Bardot took a small supporting role as Helen's servant. The director was the distinguished American Robert Wise, who had edited Orson Welles's masterpiece *Citizen Kane* (1941). Wise was the first in what was to be a long line of American directors who found themselves impressed by Baker. Startlingly, Ellen Baker recalls that Wise would subsequently offer the leading male role in *The Sound of Music* to Baker but he decided against it. Stanley seems to have found the whole experience highly entertaining, as he told Clive James: 'First of all *Helen of Troy* was directed by Robert Wise who was a very good director. I played Achilles. Again it was a marvellous part – a heavy!'

The film is an undeniably spectacular, if superficial, adaptation of Homer's *Iliad*. Its first half focuses on the Romeo and Juliet-style doomed love affair between Paris and Helen, while the second half shifts into more conventional epic mode with an enormous battle sequence followed by the unveiling of the giant wooden horse of Troy. Baker makes an impressive entrance as we see him approaching in extreme long shot down a corridor where the other Greek nobles await him. As he arrives we move into a close-up as he tells them how much he despises them all. His character is quickly established as courageous but hot-headed, arrogant and vain. If Menelaus emerges as the story's principle villain, Stanley runs him a close second. He takes the lead in the fight scenes as the Greeks lay siege to Troy and is given one of the film's most memorable set pieces when he battles Hector. Having confirmed his vicious reputation by hacking Hector to the ground and stabbing him in front of his wife, he then drags his body behind his chariot while the Trojans rain arrows down on him (they cannot harm him as he is a partially divine creature). It's an impressive sight, although justice is eventually served when an arrow from Paris finds his vulnerable heel and he falls to his death. The role is still relatively small, but again carries sufficient interest to make his performance memorable among a large cast. In a blaze of publicity, the film opened on 26 January 1956 in fifty-six countries simultaneously. The trailer promised audiences spectacle, romance and 'Bacchanalian revels of unsurpassed debauchery', as well as providing a glimpse of the 'invincible Achilles'. Box office was reasonable but, perhaps unsurprisingly, the critics weren't terribly impressed.

Richard III (1955) offered a much smaller role to Baker, but in a considerably more prestigious and artistically ambitious venture. It was to be the third of Laurence Olivier's Shakespeare adaptations following on from his patriotic wartime *Henry V* (1944) and the more introspective, Freudian-inflected version of *Hamlet* (1948). The film was financed by Alexander Korda's London Films; Stanley had signed a contract with the Hungarian-born Korda in the autumn of 1953, the year before *Richard III* went into production. Baker was happy enough to be allied to the charismatic mercurial Korda who had, over a period of twenty years, been one of the most adventurous and successful of British producers. He was joining the likes of Olivier, Eric Portman and Ralph Richardson, who were all on Korda's books. Ellen remembers her husband being impressed with Korda: 'He made actors feel safe and secure with him. Whatever his own plans, he always put their careers first and wanted them to succeed.' This was apparent in the way he allowed his contract actors to appear in projects for other producers. As a result, Baker made only a few films directly for Korda's own companies, but appeared in a number of American-backed projects in the mid 1950s. Korda was also famously generous to his actors, ensuring that they were paid well.

Richard III was an outstanding project to be involved in (eventually winning the BAFTA as best film of its year) and its location work again took Stanley abroad, this time to Spain where the Battle of Bosworth was to be filmed; rather bizarrely, Olivier claimed that he couldn't find a suitable British location and settled instead on Spain, despite the fact that the battle then appears to take place in a sun-blanched landscape with high mountains in the distance. The film adopts a deliberately theatrical, stylised approach, from the superb sets by Roger Furse to Olivier's own memorable performance as Richard. He modelled his evil monarch on cartoon drawings of the Big Bad Wolf (the reason for the false nose) and clearly relishes every line of melodramatic villainy. Baker seems to have been cast as Richmond because Olivier wanted specifically to play on his Welshness. John Wilders, the former governor of the Royal Shakespeare Company, has suggested that there was a historical pattern of Wales coming to the aid of England which can be found in several Shakespeare plays, including *Henry V* and *Cymbeline*, hence Olivier's desire to have an actor who could give Richmond an authentic Welsh accent. It is pleasant to imagine the ironic smile this argument might have solicited from Baker. It is also a happy change to see Baker cast in a heroic role, here as England's saviour from Richard's malevolence. Although the role is exceedingly brief, and reduced considerably from the play which gives Richmond two more speeches of substance, Baker again makes a striking entrance. It is Lord Stanley (Laurence Naismith) who first sees him as he approaches his tent smiling in recognition. Emblems of Wales are all around, on his tent and his chest, in the form of a red dragon. He is tall and imposing, and when he speaks it is a real pleasure to finally hear his Welsh accent. Things had moved on from the painful dubbing of *The Red Beret*. He retains just the one speech of importance when he prays before the final battle and he delivers it with quiet authority.

In his television interview with Clive James, Baker talked in some detail about the making of *Richard III*, first describing how he came to be cast:

> Up until this time I'd been playing all the heavies and all the villains in films. I had a contract with Alexander Korda who produced that picture and one day I had a call to say I want you to come in to the office and meet Laurence Olivier. I met him and he said 'I've seen two of the films you have made and one thing I must tell you as an actor is the easiest parts to play are the villains' and I recognised that because they *are* easy to play. He said the hardest thing to do as an actor is to stand up with a suit of white armour on waving a Union Jack or the Cross of St George and cry 'God for England, Harry and . . .' and I said I seem to recognise that. He said I'm going to ask you to do that because I want you to play Richmond in *Richard III* because I think you can do it. I was delighted.

He also describes the pleasure he took in being able to play Richmond with a Welsh accent, especially as he is more commonly played as a character who speaks like a public schoolboy and is 'the captain of the rugger fifteen'. Playing the role helped him start to formulate his own plans to distance himself from the villainous roles he had been playing, although the fruition of this was still a couple of years away. Curiously, Baker describes Olivier setting up a complex tracking shot in which Richmond is seen being crowned as king and over which they disagreed. The shot doesn't appear at all in the final version as we don't actually see Richmond crowned. Instead the camera stays on Olivier's Richard.

The film suffered a rather strange fate on its initial release. Korda came up with the idea of selling the film to the American television giant NBC for $500,000. They broadcast it on the same afternoon in March 1956 that it opened nationwide in American cinemas. The television version was edited for length, cropped from its original widescreen Vistavision print, and broadcast in black and white instead of Technicolor. The broadcast, which was watched by more than sixty million viewers, seriously damaged its box office receipts which were disappointing. This failure may have been instrumental in ending Olivier's ambitions to film any further Shakespeare plays; he had long nurtured the idea of filming *Macbeth* but this never came about. *Richard III* is now rightly recognised as one of the finest filmed versions of Shakespeare.

It was back to yet more dastardly deeds for Stanley on his fourth costume epic in as many years, *Alexander the Great* (1956). This was planned as a substantial Hollywood project which would combine epic production values with a more serious approach to its subject than was usually expected of the genre. It was also an important vehicle for its star, Stanley's old friend Richard Burton, whose growing status in Hollywood was hopefully to be confirmed by the film. It was also very much the personal project of its Oscar-winning writer producer and director, Robert Rossen, who had developed the idea over a number of years. It would be shot on location in Spain between February and July of 1956. Burton had sufficient clout to bring a small entourage of his friends and family to the shoot, and it's likely that it was through him that Baker was given his role. A good time was evidently had by all, particularly Burton who was by then having an affair with his co-star Claire Bloom. Despite the serious intentions, the film was a disaster at the box office and seriously damaged Burton's reputation with the studios. He, as the focal point for the film, was assumed to be principally to blame for its failure. He said of the film himself: 'I know all "epics" are awful, but I thought *Alexander the Great* might be the first good one. I was wrong.'

Looking at the film in retrospect, although it is far from the weighty project Burton had in mind, it isn't quite as poor as his assessment suggests. The first half of the film, which focuses on the political intrigues in the court of Philip of Macedonia (Frederic March), is probably closer to what both Rossen and Burton intended. It is slightly reminiscent of the BBC's later television adaptation of Robert Graves's *I, Claudius* in its attempts to uncover the motivations of the young Alexander, and his decidedly oedipal relationship with his father and mother (Olympias is played by French actress Danielle Darrieux). The second half degenerates into a seemingly endless series of battles, so that by the time we reach the admittedly spectacular confrontation with the Persians the audience is likely to be as weary as Alexander's foot soldiers. There is repeated use of one of Hollywood's clumsiest narrative devices when Alexander's progress is indicated by the camera tracking across a map while montages of battle scenes are superimposed on top. Unsurprisingly, the focus is on Burton who, despite an unfortunate wig, is athletic, handsome and in fine voice. Baker is given his usual villainous supporting role as Attalus, Philip's second-in-command, who hankers after greater power. He fares a little worse in this film than in his other costume roles of the mid 1950s, often relegated to the back of shots looking sinister. He isn't aided by the fact that a period of many years elapses in the story between his first two appearances, seemingly without him aging.

35

However, he is given one memorable scene when he brawls with Burton, something which might have brought back a few memories of their time together in London as youngsters. The film is, as ever, bolstered again by a roster of British actors including Harry Andrews and Niall MacGinnis, but it's Peter Cushing who makes most impact here with a subtly drawn performance. Looking back on these films Baker was philosophical: 'I don't regret the passing of those kinds of films. I think that possibly they were right for their time, but I don't think they would be right for 1972. I think that films and audiences have progressed a great deal since that time and people and filmmakers are more serious and pertinent now than they were then.'

Baker's typecasting in period costume films spilled over into his television work of the mid 1950s. He continued to work occasionally for the small screen where his rising status in feature films seems to have persuaded the BBC to offer him more prominent roles. For television he took two leading parts at this time which were more substantial than anything he was being given in films. *The Creature* (1955) was a ninety-minute drama about the abominable snowman written by one of the BBC's most exciting talents, Nigel Kneale. Baker took a central role opposite Peter Cushing and Eric Pohlmann in an atmospheric, unnerving production. It benefits from Neale's thoughtful writing, and all the performances are convincing. Cushing was to appear in a film version, *The Abominable Snowman* (1957), made by Hammer which didn't disgrace the original. More significant was Baker's role in the BBC's prestige six-part adaptation of Charlotte Bronte's *Jane Eyre* (1956) where he played Rochester. The series was one of the BBC's flagship productions of its year and proved a considerable success with critics and in terms of audience ratings. Although Baker is rather young at twenty-eight to play a man ten years older, he made a suitably seductive, forceful Rochester during the first half of the story, with just a hint of underlying menace. In the final scenes, as a blind, scarred figure, he extracts every grain of pathos from the part. It's a powerful performance which shows a depth and range he was rarely allowed to demonstrate in his film roles. These television appearances also brought him into millions of homes, helping to make those dark, saturnine features recognisable to a larger British audience.

By the mid 1950s another element had begun to appear in his screen persona which would prove to be more significant for his later development than his villainous roles in togas; that of the sympathetic tough guy. The first real evidence of this was in *The Good Die Young* (1954), made by the production company Romulus. Romulus was the brainchild of the entrepreneurial producers James and John Woolf. These Eton-educated brothers had begun in the industry working in distribution but moved into production in the early 1950s as a result of their disillusionment with the poor quality product they felt they were receiving from British companies. Their objective was to make films which could be sold outsidethe domestic British market, particularly in America, to which end they brought in American stars and directors to work in the UK. They had already achieved some success using this policy with two films directed by John Huston: *The African Queen* (1951) and *Moulin Rouge* (1953). The consequences of their approach are also apparent in *The Good Die Young* which features three American stars: Richard Basehart, John Ireland, and Gloria Grahame. The film also earbears a passing resemblance to the American film noir genre, a fact established from its opening shots of a gang of four desperate men driving a stolen car through night-time city streets glistening with rain. In classic noir style, we then go back in time (with the assistance of a voiceover) to discover how they came to be in this situation in the first place.

There are other noirish aspects to the film. Its realistic elements, such as a number of strikingly photographed street scenes and the authentically tough-looking boxing sequence, are combined with highly stylised sections, particularly the final chase across a graveyard and through the tunnels of the London underground. The ending has the moral tone of classic noir, as our four wrongdoers are brought to their just end as a result of their own weaknesses and greed. The film boasts impressive technical standards throughout, with cinematography by Jack Asher and art direction from Bernard Robinson, both of whom would go on to work for Hammer. The music is by the French composer Georges Auric and future director Jack Clayton was in overall charge of the production. Lewis Gilbert, whose later credits include *Alfie* (1966) and three of the Bond films, directed and co-wrote. The film benefits from a remarkably strong cast, with Margaret Leighton and a very young Joan Collins in key supporting roles, as well as a cameo from Robert Morley. At the centre of the film is a telling performance from the frequently maligned Laurence Harvey who is cast perfectly here as 'Rave' Ravenscourt, a vain, philandering upper-class cad who is finally revealed to be a gun-toting psychopath. His combination of suave good looks, ambition and unpleasantness appears not to have been too far from the private reality. Ellen Baker recalls that Harvey made life on set difficult for all concerned with his petulance and his petty demands; in the frequent scenes which take place in a pub, Harvey insisted on being served with chilled white wine which had to be precisely at the right temperature. This behaviour was employed to emphasise his star status on the film. The fact that he was also involved in a more personal way with one of his co-stars, as well as with one of the film's producers, only increased the tension on set. In an act which turned out to be unique in his career, the usually pragmatic

Baker finally had enough and, as Ellen remembers it, walked off the set. After calming down, he recovered his normal professionalism and rejoined the shoot. It's easy to imagine the clash of temperaments between the urbane Harvey and the driven, proletarian Baker. The tensions here can be seen as a precursor for the way Baker's character was to be used creatively by directors like Joseph Losey.

Despite his seventh billing, Baker is given the most interesting role of his film career to date. As Mike Morgan, a ring-weary prize fighter, he is provided with a character who generates considerable sympathy. Having saved enough money to retire from the game, Morgan suffers the loss of a hand after winning his last bout fighting while it was broken. To add to his woes, his wife lends their savings to her unreliable brother for his bail money and he then promptly flees the country. The scene in which his wife reveals the truth of their situation provides Baker with his best acting opportunity. As he breaks down with the realisation that all his suffering in the ring has been for nothing, director Lewis Gilbert heightens the emotional impact with expressionistic lighting effects and extreme camera angles. There is a real sense of the vulnerability of the character beneath his hardened exterior. Baker is convincing enough as a boxer, his angular, heavy features look the part and appropriately enough he had been an outstanding boxing prospect as a youngster himself. Audience sympathy for his character is brought to the fore at the end of the film when, in the middle of a bungled post office robbery, he decides to give himself up to the police only to be shot in the back by the murderous Ravenscourt. With his familiar toughness softened by pathos and strengthened by a sense of moral integrity, Baker was laying the foundations for his roles later in the decade.

Although well down the billing, the posters used for the British publicity campaign feature Baker's image quite prominently (in his boxing gear, clutching his injured hand), although unsurprisingly it is Laurence Harvey who is the centre of attention. British critics didn't think much of the film and some objected strongly to what they saw as its nastiness. The pessimistic violence of its final scenes seems to have placed it into the category of low-life crime film which many critics of the period were not keen to encourage. A spate of so-called 'spiv' films had appeared in the immediate postwar era and proved popular with audiences. They can now be seen as a fascinating historical phenomenon, pointing to then current anxieties about the country's moral decline and, in particular, to public concerns about juvenile delinquency. This is central to *The Good Die Young* as two of the characters are ex-servicemen and the other is still in the US Air Force. The problems of postwar readjustment to civilian life, as well as feelings of resentment over the lack of public appreciation for the sacrifices made, are themes conveyed through Richard Basehart's character, Joe Halsey, who returns from Korea to find himself out of work and in marital difficulties. If these elements seem pertinent now, contemporary British critics appear to have been more concerned about the negative image these films might create abroad. However, virtually all of the reviewers picked out Baker's performance for praise, commenting on his ability to make his character emotionally engaging. Paul Dehn in the *News Chronicle* is typical when he described it as a 'really moving performance'.

Baker made three other films while under contract to Korda, none of which added greatly to his reputation or development as an actor, but they do give an indication of the life of a jobbing actor in steady employment within the studio system of that time. Ellen suggests it was a happy time for him, in contrast with the struggles he had experienced at the beginning of the 1950s when he was finding it difficult to get anything other than walk-ons. He now found himself 'bouncing from film to film', as she put it, and usually in supporting roles of reasonable importance. *Beautiful Stranger* (1954) was a curiosity. It was produced by Marksman, a small independent company established by Maxwell Setton and John R. Sloan, and was distributed by British Lion (where Korda was effectively in charge). British Lion, which was in receivership but kept afloat by government loans, acted as an outlet for a variety of modest, low-budget producers who could use its facilities at Shepperton and release films through its distribution arm. The film itself was a crime melodrama designed as a vehicle for the declining Hollywood star Ginger Rogers. The complex narrative has Rogers's character living on the French Riviera with Baker's married businessman who, it turns out, is actually an international criminal. Herbert Lom appears as a confidence trickster who eventually murders Baker's character, and French actor Jacques Bergerac is the hero who eventually rescues Rogers. The imported American director David Miller handles the drama in a perfunctory manner, making little use of the settings, and the whole film has a sorry, neglected feel to it. Baker does his professional best with a part for which he seems ill suited, particularly as he is required to appear a good deal older than he actually is in order to make him a credible lover for Rogers. This is achieved none too convincingly by some grey streaks in the hair.

Child in the House (1956), made by B-movie specialists Eros, is principally memorable for teaming Baker with the American-born director Cy Endfield for the first time. Endfield was to become a significant figure in Baker's later career, but this wasn't a particularly auspicious start. Endfield had arrived in Britain in an attempt to escape the attentions of Senator McCarthy's anti-communist witch-hunt in Hollywood and initially made the film under the name of another director, Charles de la Tour, who acted as a 'front'. The film was eventually released under the name C. Raker Endfield. It is a sentimental family drama featuring the popular child star Mandy Miller as a young girl temporarily orphaned when her father goes on the run from the police and her mother is taken ill. She goes to the home of her aunt and uncle (Phyllis Calvert and Eric Portman) where she brings warmth into their cold lives. Baker is inevitably cast as the errant father, albeit a devoted one.

A Hill in Korea (1956), produced by Ian Dalrymple's Wessex Films and again distributed by British Lion, was the first British film to be set in the Korean War and is a more substantial piece of work. The film adopts a downbeat, realistic approach, with the familiar mix of heroics and tragedy that audiences had come to expect from the British war film. The emphasis is mainly on action, separated by sequences of rough-edged dialogue as a British patrol finds themselves cut off behind enemy lines. The film has an impressive line-up of acting talent, including future stars Robert Shaw and Michael Caine, as well as George Baker as the well-meaning but naive officer and Harry Andrews as the tough, experienced sergeant. The neatly handled battle scenes are, unfortunately, let down by the clichéd writing and threadbare production values. Most disappointing of all, Baker is cast again as the villain of the piece. His Corporal Ryker is a borderline psychopath who gets rather too much enjoyment out of killing innocent Korean civilians before being shot himself by the Chinese. In between, he spends his time threatening to kill his fellow soldiers, his barely suppressed violence causing him to break out in a stutter. Baker brings his usual conviction to the part, but by now there was something wearying about the regularity with which he was appearing in these typecast roles.

Baker kept up a remarkable work rate during this early stage of his career. Between the winter of 1952 and the middle of 1956, a period of less than four years, he had made eleven feature films and one short, as well as appearing in two major television productions. In eight of the eleven films he is cast as a villain, the only exceptions being *The Red Beret*, *The Good Die Young*, and *Richard III*. The majority of the films are relatively routine commercial productions and he is always cast in supporting roles, with only *The Cruel Sea* and *The Good Die Young* providing him with the combination of a strong part *and* a memorable film. Nonetheless, he had established himself as a reliable performer trusted by the industry and had made himself recognisable to domestic and American audiences as British cinema's current villain of choice. But why always the villain? Clearly his dark, brooding features played their part, but there was already something of the outsider about Baker within the context of British cinema. His working-class origins were central to this and his Welshness may have contributed as well; for a predominantly English, middle-class industry Baker must have seemed an oddity and was, as a result, typecast in these disruptive roles. However, as the decade progressed and British society began to experience radical changes these same qualities would turn him into a star. Fortunes were about to alter dramatically for Baker himself. On 23 January 1956 Alexander Korda died and when the dust had settled on his business affairs Stanley Baker found that, along with a number of Korda's other contracted stars, he had been 'sold' to the Rank Organisation.

CHAPTER THREE

Becoming a Tough Guy

As a Rank contract player Stanley Baker was joining the single largest organisation in the British film industry. The company had been developed in the 1930s and 1940s by its founder, J. Arthur Rank, and had grown into a vertically integrated conglomerate which dominated British films for the best part of thirty years. Rank himself could hardly have been more different to Baker's previous boss, Alexander Korda. If Korda was urbane, sophisticated, charming and cosmopolitan, then Rank was a comparatively colourless, unprepossessing figure who had been raised as a Methodist and was heir to a fortune made by his father's flour business. Rank's initial interest in films had been aroused by their possible use for religious education. Whatever his personal shortcomings, he had, by the mid 1940s, overseen the construction of an empire that included five studios, among them Pinewood and Denham (the latter having been built and then lost by Korda), a distribution company, more than 650 cinemas (including the Odeon chain), and a 'charm school' where young leading players were trained in the skills appropriate to maintaining the company's good public name.

In the 1940s Rank had operated a fairly indulgent policy towards his filmmakers. Using the company's distribution and exhibition outlets, as well as its studio facilities, he provided a safe framework in which individual directors and producers could operate on a semi-independent basis with comparatively little interference from head office. This climate had produced some of British cinema's most innovative and memorable achievements to date, including landmark work from major filmmakers such as Launder and Gilliat, David Lean, and Powell and Pressburger, as well as the classic Ealing comedies and the Gainsborough costume melodramas. However, by the time Baker became an employee in 1956 the climate had changed considerably.

By the early 1950s the Rank Organisation was in financial difficulties. An ill-fated attempt to aim films at the American market had been an expensive failure, while British audiences continued to prefer Hollywood's products to home-grown offerings. Taxes imposed by Clement Attlee's postwar government on American films shown in Britain hadn't helped Rank's chances of success in America. Under the eagle eye of his accountant, John Davis, the company underwent a painful process of rationalisation, cutting its production costs and making more modest films aimed squarely at a domestic audience. Rank became increasingly associated with tame comedies like the *Doctor in the House* series featuring Dirk Bogarde or nostalgic Second World War adventures starring Kenneth More or Richard Todd. It was a different climate to the one Baker had experienced under Korda where actors were treated with consideration and allowed a degree of freedom. Rank's contract players were told in no uncertain terms what was expected of them. Ellen Baker recalls vividly the annual Rank Christmas party at the Dorchester where John Davis would publicly announce the forthcoming production plans for the year and indicate the films which its stars, directors and other personnel were likely to appear in. With the exception of Dirk Bogarde and Kenneth More, who tended to be favoured with the strongest roles, the other actors inevitably left under a cloud of depression at the routine fare they were going to have to take part in. She remembers only Peter Finch openly rebelling by letting Davis know precisely what he thought of the material Rank had in store for him.

The situation wasn't aided by the fact that Rank made it apparent that they didn't see Baker as a leading man but strictly as a supporting player. Ellen recalls that they specifically felt that he couldn't be cast in a role which required him to carry a romantic storyline; he simply didn't fit in with Rank's idea of what a romantic leading man should be. Considering that their ideal personification of this role was Bogarde or Anthony Steel it is easy to see why Baker was considered too unconventional to be a leading man. With binding contracts that effectively made actors slaves to the studio management, there was little that Baker could do. The notion of someone being 'sold' to another employer, as Baker had been when Korda died and his contract was passed on to Rank, may seem unthinkable now but was standard practice in an industry which viewed stars largely as commodities. As part of Rank's publicity operation, Baker was now required to attend royal film premieres, be photographed about town with young Rank starlets and be a judge at seaside beauty pageants. One Pathé newsreel shows him looking decidedly uncomfortable as he helps to crown Miss New Brighton 1956. It was all in a day's work for a Rank contract player.

Considering Rank's view of Baker's abilities, he could hardly have been surprised to find that he was going to make his Rank debut cast again as the villain. This was to be in a crime thriller set around the world of motor racing called *Checkpoint* (1956). It was made by one of Rank's most reliable production teams, led by producer Betty Box with Ralph Thomas directing and a script by Robin Estridge. Box was a remarkable figure in British cinema, being virtually the only woman producer working in the industry. She had built a reputation for making solid commercial films which could virtually guarantee a reasonable size audience. With Ralph Thomas she produced thirty-odd films including their most successful franchise, the *Doctor in the House* series which they had started in 1954. The Box–Thomas team could turn their hands to most genres, but it's not unfair to suggest that their work was more often efficient rather than particularly original. *Checkpoint* was an unusually ambitious project, shot largely on location in Italy in Eastmancolor with the collaboration of Aston Martin who provided the cars for the impressive racing scenes. At the very least, it provided another expenses-paid trip for Stanley to an attractive location.

The film is in many respects typical mid-1950s genre filmmaking. Little care has been taken with the formulaic plot and stock characters. Instead the emphasis is on the picturesque locales and even prettier cars. Rank's young heart-throb Anthony Steel has the lead with characteristic support from Michael Medwin and James Robertson Justice. Baker is cast as O'Donovan, a ruthless, immoral conman who steals the blueprint for the 'Volta new fuel intake' and manages to blow up a car plant in the process, killing five policemen and the amiable, elderly nightwatchman. As ever, he tackles the part with relish, exuding tight-lipped menace. His social politeness masks an uncertainly controlled aggression which is genuinely unnerving. David Berry, the historian of Welsh cinema, puts it beautifully when he says that 'Baker seemed to carry into his roles the tetchiness, restlessness and defence mechanisms developed in his harsh early years as a miner's son in the Rhondda valley.' There is also something reminiscent of Lee Marvin's version of the 'heavy' role apparent in the impression that Baker might explode into violence at any moment. As in a number of his previous films, this contrasts strikingly with the bland performance of Anthony Steel. However, nothing can really lift the film out of its clichéd presentation of the jet set lifestyle of the drivers. The sometimes unintentionally humorous dialogue includes such gems as Steel's pronouncement that 'women are as tricky as the devil and best driven fast'.

He fared a little better with *Campbell's Kingdom* (1957), which was made by the same team of Betty Box, Ralph Thomas and Robin Estridge, and adapted from a novel by Hammond Innes. This at least has the curiosity value of being that rarest of beasts, a British western. Set in the Canadian Rockies but filmed on location in Spain and in the studios at Pinewood, it stars Dirk Bogarde as Bruce Campbell, a man who has been diagnosed (incorrectly) with a terminal illness and who inherits a tract of wild land which may just contain oil. He finds himself in a race against time with the dastardly Owen Morgan, played by Baker, who wants to build a dam and flood the whole area. The film has the same ambitious production values as *Checkpoint*, being shot in Eastmancolor and providing a series of pyrotechnic stunts including the blowing up of a bridge and the final destruction of the dam. The eccentric casting includes John Laurie, Finlay Currie, Sid James (as a nervous truck driver), and James Robertson Justice who adopts an impenetrable Scottish brogue. The various attempts at Canadian accents don't help proceedings, although Baker manages to be more convincing than most. The western genre elements are established from the opening as we see Michael Craig riding out across a snowy, mountainous landscape, and when Bogarde arrives in the main hotel/saloon where the suspicious locals greet him with stony silence.

Baker seems even more in his element here, swaggering about in his black cowboy hat and red shirt, glowering from under those dark brows and chewing on a cheroot; he resembles a villain from a spaghetti western. In contrast, Bogarde looks ill –at ease in his part. With his refined English accent and gentle manner, he is less than convincing as he charges round the mountains blowing up roads and excavating for oil. There is something incongruous as he walks about the frontier town in his camelhair coat with his hands folded behind his back, like a gentleman farmer out for a Sunday stroll. However, the scenes between the two of them have a surprising charge. There is a palpable air of antagonism between the two which was to re-emerge to more substantial effect in *Accident* (1967) ten years later. Ellen Baker recalls that this on-screen spark stemmed in part from a less than agreeable relationship behind the scenes during the filming. Bogarde had not greatly endeared himself to the cast by declining to socialise with them after the daily shoot. He preferred to spend most of his spare time visiting the set of a big-budget Hollywood film which was being shot nearby by the director John Huston.

Ellen enjoys recounting a number of stories about the making of *Campbell's Kingdom*. Stanley enjoyed gambling and had invited Huston, who had similar tastes, to come for a weekend of poker with other members of the cast. Huston happily agreed but subsequently had to call off when he was removed from his film. As a parting gift, he sent wine whisky and cigars to compensate for his absence. She also tells an embarrassing but comic yarn that perhaps says something of Bogarde's attitude towards his own star status. The cast had been afflicted by crabs, caused when less than the expected care had been taken with the hygiene of their costumes. All costumes and clothing had to go for cleaning. Encountering Bogarde's friend and manager Anthony Forwood, heading out of their hotel with

Bogarde's apparel, the Bakers enquired if poor Dirk had been stricken with the same affliction as everyone else, only be told by an indignant Forwood that it was nothing of the kind; Dirk had become so fit on the rugged location that his consequent weight loss required his clothes to be taken in. Whatever the source of the tensions between Baker and Bogarde, it certainly adds considerably to the effectiveness of their encounters on screen.

The film which finally marked a decisive shift in Baker's career was *Hell Drivers* (1957). Increasingly frustrated and disillusioned with Rank's treatment of him, this was a project which Baker became involved with in a more personal way. Its origins lay in a story by the writer John Kruse who had spent some time working as a lorry driver and then used these experiences as the basis for the story's setting. Director Cy Endfield worked with Kruse on developing this into a screenplay and then shot the film under the name C. Raker Endfield for the small independent company Aqua, with financial backing and distribution from Rank. Endfield had enjoyed working with Baker on *A Child in the House* and seems to have thought of him immediately for the central role of Tom Yately. As well as being made at arm's length from the main Rank set-up, the film offered Baker the chance to play the lead role, a sympathetic tough guy character who was to carry the film's romantic subplot, as well as supplying the obligatory heroics. By stepping down into a smaller-scale, lower status production, Baker conversely gave himself the chance of a more substantial part and a change of direction in terms of his screen persona. It was a calculated gamble but one which was to pay off. Ellen remembers that Rank was far from happy with the project, wanting Stanley cast in a supporting role. It's certainly possible to imagine him playing the brutish Red, a part eventually given to Patrick McGoohan. She recalls how Stanley threatened to walk out if he didn't get the lead. It was a rare instance of Baker not doing as he was told by his employers, but he seems to have sensed how crucial the opportunity was for him.

The film has subsequently developed something of a cult reputation which seems, in retrospect, deserved. It unquestionably stands out from anything else Baker had done to this point. To begin with, the casting is remarkable. As well as Baker and McGoohan, there is William Hartnell (the future Dr Who) as the corrupt chief of a haulage firm employing a gang of short-haul drivers which includes Herbert Lom, Alfie Bass, Sid James, Gordon Jackson and a very young Sean Connery (who slept for a while on the floor of the Bakers' home as he had nowhere else to live at the time). Baker's young brother is played by David McCallum and the film's love interest is provided by a combination of Peggy Cummins and Jill Ireland. It was an exceptional combination of old hands and new faces, some of whom were going to play a substantial part in changing the face of British cinema and television in the next decade. The film combines surface realism with a visual panache rare in British action pictures of the period. The realism, which seems to foreshadow the techniques of the New Wave 'kitchen sink' films by at least a couple of years, is provided by the extensive location shooting and the grainy cinematography of Geoffrey Unsworth, who would later work with Stanley Kubrick. Rarely had a 1950s British genre film looked so grimly authentic. The visual panache is evident in the style with which the American-born Endfield handles proceedings. Film noir lighting is used in a number of sequences to add atmosphere and the driving scenes make considerable use of point-of-view shots to convey the excitement of the trucks careering around the English countryside. Even the static shots of Baker in the cab of his lorry are made visually arresting by the use of extreme close-ups and low angles to emphasise the intensity of his perform-ance. The film is directed with an energy economy and dynamism which has more in common with American B- movies than standard British produc-tions of the time.

This distinctly American quality also extends to Baker's performance. When we first see him he is photographed from behind as he approaches the haulage yard. Wearing a leather flight jacket he could easily be mistaken for Robert Mitchum or William Holden. The film supplies him with a series of terse one-liners and his relationship with Peggy Cummins crackles with sexual tension. When he finally kisses her it's hardly the decorous embrace of a typical British hero; instead he swoops on her neck like a vampire and the lights are quickly dimmed to save the audience's blushes. There is a palpable sense of antagonism between Baker and McGoohan which explodes into an unusually convincing fistfight. In a promotional interview Baker revealed that McGoohan, like himself, had personal experience of boxing and that Endfield had encouraged the two of them to actually fight with each other in the sequence. Whether it was the combination of Celtic temperaments or just the testosterone-fuelled nature of the film, Baker and McGoohan reach a near demented level of aggression. Ellen remembers McGoohan as a difficult, driven performer who threatened to walk off the film himself. Baker is convincingly tough, but the film also allows the audience to see the gentle, warmer side to his persona. This can be found in his scenes with Herbert Lom's Gino, the Italian Catholic who takes a liking to Baker's character and forges a friendship with him. The film is also careful to suggest a degree of vulnerability in Baker, apparent in the guilt he feels when he returns to the family shop to speak to the younger brother who has been seriously injured as a result of Baker's errant ways. His personal moral code is shown when he takes on Hartnell's corrupt owner on behalf of all the drivers. For the first time, Baker was given a role which encouraged audiences to identify with a complex but ruggedly masculine figure.

Rank's publicity department went into overdrive in selling the film, playing heavily on its more lurid elements of violence and brutality. The main poster promises us 'A fight to the death and the weapons are ten-ton trucks!' accompanied by images of a grimacing Baker, while the trailer boasted that there was 'death at every bend'. Theatre managers were encouraged by Rank to match the aggression of the film with equally punchy promotional campaigns: 'Publicised a real "meaty" picture lately? If not, here's one you can certainly get your teeth into. "Hell Drivers" is a tough, gripping film which will keep audiences on the edge of their seats. Your publicity should be equally forceful.' They were even offered a set of stills graphically detailing the punch-up between Baker and McGoohan and a five-part cartoon strip serialisation which could be issued to local newspapers. A promotional short film, *Look in on Hell Drivers*, was at pains to illustrate the film's authenticity (while not suggesting that all haulage companies operated along the lines of the one shown in the film). We see some real lorry drivers vouching to the film's accuracy and meet Cy Endfield wading through a sea of mud on the film's main location, an industrial sand pit. Alfie Bass is spotted eating his lunch perched on an overturned barrel and regales us with stories of his own experiences working in various manual jobs. The presenter, Michael Ingrams, informs us that it's difficult to tell the actors from the real workers on the site, emphasising that this film's stars are as tough as the real thing.

Although the critics were startled by the film's melodramatic content, the reviews were almost uniformly good, with many commenting that it was a British tough-guy film which could, for once, stand up to what American cinema offered in this line. Some suggested that it resembled a western. As the *Sunday Times* reviewer put it, *Hell Drivers* was 'a well-made, exciting, tough film with a pace and a masculine command of violent action uncommon in the British cinema'. Baker, McGoohan and Enfield were all praised by a range of newspapers and magazines. Only the solemn reviewer for the British Film Institute's *Monthly Film Bulletin* seemed to misjudge the film. The (very) brief review is worth quoting in full:

> This extraordinary film may interest future historians for its description of road haulage and masculine social behaviour in the mid-twentieth century; perhaps fortunately, however, it is so unconvincing in every respect that even the most gullible could not accept it as a representative picture of either. There are some good individual acting performances, but the film, though produced with efficiency and assurance, is disagreeable and occasionally vicious.

Rank could hardly have asked for a better endorsement or one more likely to bring in the crowds. The film has continued to attract critical and academic attention, most recently in an essay by Elisabetta Girelli in the American *Cinema Journal* which considered the portrayal of Gino as a specifically Italian tough guy.

The gradual transformation of Baker's screen persona which *Hell Drivers* started has been the subject of discussion by film historians. In Andrew Spicer's essay 'The Emergence of the British Tough Guy: Stanley Baker, Masculinity and the Crime Thriller', the author places Baker's new persona in the context of British and American crime films of the period. Spicer identifies the 'tough guy' as a character typically marked by his harsh upbringing, who then uses the resilience that this has given him to make his way in the world. He is streetwise, determined and willing to bend the rules, but possessed of a strong moral code. For Spicer, this character type is a staple of American cinema where he represents a version of the American ideal of self-improvement and self-reliance, but at this point was largely unknown in British cinema where the 'gentleman' was the more dominant type. The 'gentleman' didn't need to be tough as the privileges of the British class system gave him a position of authority, 'his metier was restraint, moral authority and the preservation of the status quo'.

For Geoffrey Macnab, it is precisely this context which makes Baker's emergence so striking and which accounts for his impact:

> It's an indictment of that period that the 'chaps', well bred and in their flannel trousers, still monopolised most of the leading roles. Bogarde was offering his endless reprises of Simon Sparrow in the *Doctor* series, Kenneth More and John Gregson were hooting their way down to Brighton in their antique cars, Jack Hawkins was looking suitably sagacious, but there was no room for Stanley Baker in the league of gentlemen. He was down in the basement, playing the thugs and heavies, and might never have been given the chance to come up and show his true mettle had it not been for Senator McCarthy and the House Committee on un-American Activities.

The latter is obviously a reference to the part played in Baker's development by the two expatriate American directors Cy Endfield and Joseph Losey, both of whom came to Britain to escape the McCarthy witch-hunts.

Spicer links the appearance of the British tough guy to wider changes occurring in Britain in the late 1940s and 1950s. As he puts it, 'the dislocations of the war and the problems of readjustment were refracted in a spate of crime films produced in the immediate postwar period, particularly a cycle of "spiv" films, urban thrillers with London settings.' These films gave expression to a number of social anxieties, particularly in relation to youth crime and the dangers posed to national stability by working-class criminality.

They were also a vehicle for the appearance of a new kind of popular hero. As the promise of a newly classless postwar society failed to materialise with any speed, fissures in British society began to open up and were barely concealed by official attempts to claim an ongoing consensus. Baker's appearance in *Hell Drivers* and the films which follow it clearly hit a chord with audiences of the time. The 1950s saw the beginning of a gradual decline in cinema attendance levels from the peak of the war years. As audiences started to dwindle, the social character of the audience that remained also changed. In comparison with the war period, the audience of the 1950s and 1960s was more predominantly male, unsurprisingly enough, but it was also typically younger and working class. By the time of the release of *Hell Drivers* Britain was already experiencing the burgeoning of a youth culture typified by a less respectful attitude to the older generation and by its veneration of rebellious pop stars like Elvis Presley. British cinema needed to catch up with these developments: American cinema already had Marlon Brando and James Dean. It was clear that British audiences wanted home-grown stars who could generate the same excitement and sense of identification. The time was ripe for anti-establishment figures to emerge.

The question remains as to why Baker was so effective in these roles. His physical appearance obviously played its part in this. The lantern jaw, barrel chest and penetrating gaze suggested a man who could take care of himself. His ability to play gentle and vulnerable were then all the more striking by contrast. For Ellen Baker it was simply a matter of his not being like other British stars of the time; the tough-guy persona itself was new for British cinema. His son Martin suggests that it was the authenticity in his perform-ances that made them work: 'He felt a degree of personal identification with the working-class roles he played and felt that their popularity was due to a sense of recognition from the audience.' He didn't have to imitate a working-class upstart, as that was what he had been. Henry Cooper described him as the only British star of the period who was a 'man's man'; but there is more to his persona than just this, although the bluntly masculine side of his image was unquestionably a contrast to other British stars of the era who Cooper refers to as 'effeminate'. Baker's ability to create a British version of the classic American tough-guy persona was also a reason for his success. Apart from the fact that American directors seemed drawn to work with him, it's interesting to note the number of film historians who refer to American stars when trying to describe his appeal. For Geoffrey Macnab the comparison is with Lee Marvin and Robert Ryan. His old room-mate while with Birmingham Rep., Dennis Quilley, likened him to John Wayne and Humphrey Bogart, and Ellen suggests that he modelled himself on Robert Mitchum whom he would later befriend. For audiences, he possessed the same dynamism and democratic appeal as these blue-collar heroes.

Macnab also suggests that Baker's Welsh background was a component in creating this new persona. He places Baker in a grouping with Richard Burton and Anthony Hopkins whom he refers to as 'valley boys' (an appropriate enough description for Baker and Burton, if slightly inaccurate with Margam-born Hopkins). Macnab identifies two areas of Baker's screen image which might be attributed to his Welsh upbringing. First, there is the image of the hard-drinking brawler schooled in the rough Rhondda valley and equipped with an instinct for survival, as well as a capacity for enjoying himself. Then there is the soulful, poetic Welshman, more commonly associated with Burton or Hopkins, but potentially also applicable to Baker; a tender, romantic individual inclined to melancholy. Although it is easy to dismiss this as stereotypical imagery more likely to be found in the cinema of England or Hollywood than in Wales itself, it made for a powerful screen presence. The clash between the two sides of the image fits well with the contradictions of the tough-guy persona itself, at once tough and tender. It is interesting and appropriate that Peter Stead, writing about the contrasting acting styles of Burton and Baker, should use a sporting metaphor to sum this up, whereby the 'cool rugby back-row forward with his public school and varsity background stands in marked contrast to the gritty, aggressive, never say die centre forward from the local state school'. His Welshness can also be linked to his frequent portrayal of outsiders, bucking a system which chooses not to acknowledge them. Oddly, this Welshness is rarely directly referred to within the films themselves, with the exception of his roles in *Richard III* and *Hell Drivers*. In the latter, the other drivers notice his accent and ask him if he is from Cardiff, to which he replies that he's from Blaenllechau (actually the name of the village next door to Ferndale). Baker's pronunciation leads Sid James to remark that it sounds more like a horrible disease than a place (the most common stereotype of the Welsh in English cinema has been a comic one).

The final component in the make-up of Baker's persona was class. The British film industry of the 1950s was entrenched with middle-class personnel at virtually all levels. This was frequently reflected in the values which the films contained. A working-class actor was a comparative rarity, especially outside certain designated roles which tended to be in comedy or crime films. This again made Baker an outsider within the industry itself and a rare figure as a star. However, his class background was more in tune with the audience than virtually any other British star of the period. The working-class heroes of the New Wave were just a couple of years away and

Baker can be seen as a precursor for the likes of Albert Finney, Michael Caine and Terence Stamp. Caine himself acknowledged the debt that working-class actors like him owed to Baker in breaking the mould in British cinema. The fact that Baker himself never became part of the New Wave might be attributed to his age; at five years older than Caine and ten years older than Stamp he was less able to tap into the same youth appeal as these actors. The fact that he had been a reliable studio actor for ten years prior to their appearance also worked against him.

The new movement towards working-class stories told with a greater sense of accuracy had its origins in the theatre with the production of John Osborne's *Look Back in Anger* at the Royal Court Theatre in 1956. This was followed by a wave of successful proletarian novels like Alan Sillitoe's *Saturday Night and Sunday Morning* and John Braine's *Room at the Top*. These books and plays paved the way for film adaptations which would take British cinema into a new era. Referring to Baker, David Berry argues that 'the British New Wave cinema, inspired partly by writers like John Osborne and Alan Sillitoe, seemed tailor-made for him as they homed in on fierce class loyalties and schisms'. If Baker never became part of the New Wave itself it was because he remained at heart a film star of the old school, working within a mainstream which he was helping to change.

In Richard Dyer's book *Stars*, he outlines three dominant film star 'types'. Two of these are the 'The Good Joe' and 'The Pin-up' but the third is 'The Tough Guy'. Dyer describes this last type as having many characteristics of the conventional hero or 'Good Joe', but suggests he is distinguished by a degree of moral ambivalence: 'As a result he confuses the boundaries between good and bad behaviour, presses the antisocial into the service of the social and vice versa. In this instance, this type does not indicate collective approval, disapproval or ridicule, but confusion and ambiguity.' The 'Tough Guy' typically uses methods normally reserved for the villain but puts them towards a just cause. His motives may sometimes be flawed but in the end he does the right thing. These flaws potentially afford a greater sense of identification for an audience which might find the 'Good Joe' too clean-cut. Baker continued to develop this type in two further films made under his Rank contract, although an increasing distance was opening up between him and the studio.

The first of these was *Violent Playground* (1958), made by the director–producer team of Basil Dearden and Michael Relph with the backing of Rank. Dearden and Relph had first met on the Ealing film *The Bells Go Down* (1943) where Dearden made his debut as a director and Relph acted as his art director. Subsequently, they became the most productive filmmaking team working at Ealing, establishing a name as makers of popular genre

1. Stanley as a baby with his sister Muriel. Courtesy of Muriel Lewis.

2. Stanley with his father, Jack Baker. Courtesy of Muriel Lewis.

3. The Baker household at 16 Albany Street, Ferndale. Courtesy of Robert Shail.

THIS PLAQUE
MARKS THE BIRTHPLACE OF
STANLEY BAKER
28TH FEBRUARY 1928
DISTINGUISHED ACTOR
AND PRODUCER

4. The plaque that marks Stanley's childhood home. Courtesy of Robert Shail.

5. Stanley's mentor and teacher, Glynne Morse. Courtesy of Muriel Lewis.

8. The Royal Premiere of *The Guns of Navarone* (1961). Courtesy of Lady Ellen Baker.

9. Working-class hero: the underrated *A Prize of Arms* (1962).
British Lion/Bryanston, courtesy of the Kobal collection.

10. Typically intense in Joseph Losey's *The Criminal* (1960). Anglo Amalgamated, courtesy of the Kobal Collection.

films which combined realism with a concern for tackling social issues from a liberal standpoint. They would go on to make *Sapphire* (1959), the first mainstream British film to deal directly with issues of racial discrimination, and *Victim* (1961), which was credited with helping to bring about a relaxation in British laws dealing with homosexuality. They had already tackled juvenile delinquency in *The Blue Lamp* (1949) and returned to the theme with *Violent Playground*. The film takes a sympathetic view of the methods adopted by Liverpool's police service in trying to combat youth crime in the city via preventative measures. The subject was highly topical with Dearden and Relph entering the public debate themselves by writing an open letter to the *Sunday Times* just after the completion of the film endorsing the approach taken in Liverpool.

Violent Playground is a good illustration of the tension at the centre of much of Dearden and Relph's work within the 'social problem' genre in that its success is dependent upon finding a balance between entertainment and a progressive message. The film's promotional materials reflect this division. In a carefully staged promotional interview filmed by Rank, Baker is at pains to point out how the film reflects positively on the strategies adopted by the police in Liverpool and quotes the huge percentage drop in offences achieved by their socially aware methods. The press book issued for the film talks about Dearden and Relph's intention to tell a realistic story which will 'move your compassion', a story based on facts and concerned with methods designed to *prevent* juvenile crime (their italics). However, the poster's photographs of a concerned-looking Baker leading a child by the hand are undermined by a lurid drawing of David McCallum wielding a machine gun. The press response also reflected this division. The popular press reviewed the film as a straightforward crime movie, generally approving of its energy and style. The broadsheets roundly attacked the film for its hypocrisy, suggesting that the elements of social conscience were just an excuse to justify a violent, exploitative film. *The Times* review is fairly typical:

> A work that sets out to be no more than a piece of entertainment should be assessed as such; but if the aim of a film is to say something that matters, then it is only fitting to criticise it if it fails to do so. Here, it seems, is an English film that is going to try to say something of social importance. As the story progresses all attempts to discuss any genuine social problems are abandoned in favour of a melodramatic and improbable climax. Thus a film which sets out with such self-avowed high purposes degenerates into something that is basically dishonest, since the real issues are evaded.

The film was compared to colourful American youth concern films such as *The Blackboard Jungle* (1955) and David McCallum even found himself being compared to James Dean.

Seen now, the second half of the film certainly confirms the views of its detractors. As David McCallum's character rapidly turns from misunderstood youth into sociopath and arsonist, attempting to burn down the Grand Hotel which had previously refused him entry, the film becomes increasingly hysterical, culminating in a school siege as he holds a group of toddlers captive at gunpoint. An underlying anxiety about the corruption of British youth by the evils of pop music reaches absurd proportions, particularly in a lurid sequence where Baker is menaced by a gang of lads apparently driven half-crazed by listening to primitive rock and roll; they invite Baker to either run or stay and dance. The first half of the film is more successful, with its location sequences on the streets of Liverpool and a genuine attempt to argue for a sympathetic approach to the problems of the urban young. Baker's Sgt Truman argues that all they need is 'a whole lot of mum and a little bit of dad' to set them on the right road. Baker is given another chance to show his softer side. Although his appearance in trench coat and trilby still suggests the Americanised tough guy, it becomes apparent that he is the gentle face of authority. He tries to help the kids by taking them to a youth club and by assisting at an athletics meeting. Humour is used to make Baker's hard-man persona more approachable, particularly in his dealings with the two youngest members of the Murphy clan (played winningly by Brona and Fergal Boland) who he takes under his wing. He is also allowed to tentatively develop his romantic image in his relationship with their elder sister played by Anne Heywood. Baker's physical stature is used for once to suggest a paternalistic quality in him.

A far more interesting progression of Baker's screen image is apparent in *Blind Date* (1959), released in America as *Chance Meeting*. The increasing distance between Baker and Rank is evident in the fact that although the film was released by Rank, it was produced as a joint venture by Sydney Box Associates and the Independent Artists production company. The film is significant not least as the first occasion that Baker was to work with Joseph Losey. The American-born director had come to Britain in 1952 fleeing from the HUAC investigations which were persecuting liberals in Hollywood. *Blind Date* was his fifth British film but the first in which he seems completely in command of his subject. He had built his reputation in America through taut crime films which also expressed his political leanings. This is a pretty accurate description of *Blind Date*. The film is characteristic of Losey in the fluency of its camerawork, its complex flashback structure and the occasional use of expressionistic lighting. It also prefigures his later 1960s work in its use of a jazz score. Most typical of all is its manipulation of interior spaces. This is seen in the depiction of Jacqueline's ornately decorated flat which is introduced in a long sequence at the start of the film as Hardy Kruger wanders round its empty rooms. Even Losey's trademark use of mirrors is evident here; they are employed in a number of scenes, including one in which we see multiple images of Kruger reflected in two mirrors. Losey portrays a disorienting world where appearances are deceptive and a penniless young artist (Kruger) suddenly finds himself accused of murdering his lover. It is also a world of class hypocrisies and deceits, as he realises when he discovers that Jacqueline is really Lady Fenton, the wife of a high-ranking British diplomat who has been using him to take revenge on her philandering husband. 'It always amazes me – how mean the rich are', he comments.

Losey's political intentions are apparent in the depiction of Baker's Inspector Morgan (only the third obviously Welsh character he had played to date). Morgan uncovers the moral degeneracy of the British upper classes through the behaviour of Sir Howard and Lady Fenton, the former revealed as an adulterer and the latter as a murderer. Morgan is leaned on by his equally upper-class superiors in the police force to effectively frame Kruger so as to allow the real culprits to escape. It is clear that the ruling elite look after each other's interests. However, his working-class instincts (being the son of a chauffeur) enable him to uncover the truth, as he explains to his boss: 'Being brought up the way I was, you get to know the givers and the takers. You can smell them out. It's a question of background.' Although Baker takes second billing behind Kruger, he is able to develop his tough-guy persona further than before. His Inspector Morgan is determined, streetwise and sceptical. His willingness to use underhand methods to a worthwhile end is in line with Richard Dyer's description of the 'tough guy' type. We see this when he allows Kruger to discover the dead body of his lover just so that he can gauge his reaction. At the same time, we see that he is vulnerable and at the mercy of his own feelings. Struggling against a cold, he can't help but show his personal satisfaction when he finally unravels the mystery and gains a class victory over his 'superiors'. It is a performance bristling with class resentments.

The film was generally well received, obtaining a BAFTA nomination. One or two critics picked up on its class antagonisms and critique of Britain's ruling establishment. A number of reviewers were rather shocked by the film's sexual explicitness, something which Rank had unsurprisingly played on in its promotional posters which promised audiences 'SEX. . . as frank as life itself!' The reviewer for *The Guardian* considered it part of a new trend in British cinema, already established by the early New Wave films, towards 'toughness laced with frankness'. The film is fairly blunt for the period in indicating a relationship between a young man and an older woman in which the principal attraction is sexual. Although the critic of the *Daily Telegraph* bizarrely found Baker's mild Welsh accent impenetrable, the majority of reviewers praised his performance with Anthony Carthew in the *Daily Herald* and John Waterman in the London *Evening Standard* picking out his contribution as a key feature of the film. Len Moseley in the *Daily Express* went so far as to write a feature article suggesting that *Blind Date* was evidence that Baker had been typecast for too long and had now finally been revealed as true star material. He described Baker in effusive terms:

> He has the muscles, sinews and solidity of an oak tree. Like most Welshmen, he has the kind of milk-fed voice that can charm the birds off the trees and the rabbits out of their burrows – though when he raises it, he can also burst your eardrums. He is the handsomest and most manly-looking man in British films.'

David Berry has high praise for Baker in the film, seeing it as 'the performance of his career in the cinema' and a role which 'stamped him as distinctive in a long-moribund British cinema beginning to stir into life with the influx of American talent and money.' Peter Stead takes a similar view, describing the combination of Losey and Baker as 'a high-water mark of American and British intermingling' and the film as indicating that British cinema 'had been given a new level of resentment and a new range of class and moral perspectives.' Of all of Baker's less publicly known performances this is the one which most deserves reappraisal.

By this stage of his career, the British press had begun to pick up on Baker's change of image and were happy to recast him from the public's favourite villain to their preferred tough guy. The *News of the World* selected him for their 'Star of the Week' feature in September 1959 and introduced the article by describing Baker as 'an actor who simply doesn't conform to the usual idea of a hero'. Appropriately, the interview takes place in the 'four-ale bar of an East End pub with a bunch of cronies, all of them renowned in the boxing ring'. The article goes on to reveal that among Baker's 'cronies' is Henry Cooper. The piece paints a picture of an uncompromising working-class hero in the process of shaking up British cinema. Baker seems to have been pleased with this shift in his career; at least he was now taking the lead role in his films, even if they were smaller productions. He was also developing a consistent fan base with, according to *Films and Filming*, an increasing appeal to young women as a sex symbol. Questioned for a BBC Wales interview about the violence in his films he justifies this as part of a pursuit of greater realism. He is seems a little offended by a suggestion that he might be creating a poor role model for the young and laughs this off. He also attempts to put some distance between his private self and the on-screen persona, arguing that the edginess of his film roles is actually the antithesis of the gentle family man and hard-working actor that is the real Stanley Baker. By this time he was living comfortably in Wimbledon with Ellen and the children (their third child, Glyn, was born on 9 June 1957). This apparent contradiction between his on and off-screen life was reflected in a later interview with Ellen in *Photoplay* headlined 'Life with a Tough Guy'. She tells the reporter: 'People have got Stanley all wrong. Those who don't know him ask: "What's he like to live with – mean, moody, tough?" You see they've seen too many of his pictures and they believe what they see on the screen. But Stanley isn't like that at all. He's a big baby.' Of course, the contrast between the tough exterior and a softer underside was a crucial ingredient of the appeal of the classic tough-guy figure.

By 1959 Baker's patience with Rank had expired. He told *Films and Filming* that Rank 'have no plans as an organisation. They change attitudes week by week, almost day by day.' Over the preceding three years he had gradually edged himself to the fringes of their operation, appearing in films made by small independent companies under the Rank banner. He was also becoming increasingly independently minded himself, wanting to take greater control over the direction his career was taking. He had little faith in Rank's ability to offer him worthwhile roles. They seemingly had no belief in him and would have kept him playing heavies for the rest of his days. He took the brave decision to buy himself out of his contract, raising the not inconsiderable sum of £12,000 by borrowing it from his agent. This was a risky move, but Ellen remembers that they both had absolute confidence in his popularity with audiences and other filmmakers. They were vindicated as the offers of work continued to steadily roll in and he was able to pay his agent back within six months. The concept of the freelance star was already becoming established in Hollywood but Baker's move remained unusual in British cinema. It also placed him firmly with the new breed of young working-class actors like Albert Finney who preferred to be free agents.

One of the characteristics of the tough-guy persona according to Richard Dyer is its moral ambiguity. He may come through in the final reel but along the way he is allowed to at least consider straying from the moral path. For Dyer, this allows the audience to release their own feelings of disquiet with prevailing social values, without actually endorsing complete rebellion. The ability of stars to give voice to the audience's own anxieties tends to appear at times of social change or division. This would apply to Britain at the end of the 1950s with the radical changes of the1960s just around the corner.

Film historian Robert Murphy argues that Baker was an exception among British stars of the period in being able to give expression to these undercurrents and suggests that it is this quality which separated him from other contemporary stars like Jack Hawkins whose appeal was based on reassuring the audience rather than representing their concerns.

Baker continued to explore the possibilities of this persona in two films which he made for Hammer after leaving his Rank contract: *Yesterday's Enemy* (1959) and *Hell is a City* (1960). Hammer's reputation today rests firmly on the Gothic horror films with which they made their name but in the late 1950s they were still in the early days of pursuing that production policy. Liberally interspersed with the monster movies were a number of low-budget films covering other popular genres such as crime, science fiction, period costume romps and war subjects. Both *Yesterday's Enemy* and *Hell is a City* were made in this context. *Yesterday's Enemy* has many typical characteristics of Hammer's production style, from employing such regulars behind the camera as Arthur Grant (cinematography), James Needs (editor) and Bernard Robinson (production design), to the use of a limited number of sets as a result of the all too obviously tight budget. The latter sometimes leads to the impression that we are watching a filmed play or a television production. There is also the inclusion of a good deal of brutally violent action. The cast is full of familiar faces in supporting roles including Leo McKern as a cynical war reporter and Gordon Jackson as the hearty sergeant. The film certainly lives up to its publicity tagline, 'War is Hell', presenting the British campaign in Burma with an unrelentingly grim pessimism. Its anti-war message is startlingly explicit, as the exact purpose of the fighting we witness remains unexplained; the acts of violence consequently feel random and arbitrary. The film's sense of moral ambivalence is brought home through a neatly constructed narrative; the decision of Captain Langford (Baker) to execute two Burmese civilians in order to force a Japanese spy into divulging the secrets of an impending attack is subsequently turned around, with a Japanese officer executing British POWs to get Langford to talk. The film presents war as the ultimate irony, reducing civilised men (the Japanese officer is presented with some sympathy) to a state of barbarity.

In keeping with this, Baker's British officer is a deeply divided character. He runs his unit with unremitting harshness, exhibiting a ruthlessness which shocks his fellow officers, as when he denies morphine to dying men so that it can be saved for the injured who might recover. In classic tough-guy mode, he tells them 'I'm not concerned with the methods I use' – it is obviously only results that matter. With his execution of two civilians, any sympathy the audience has for him is stretched to the limit. And yet he is capable of acts of tenderness towards his men, and they respect his toughness as something necessary to ensure their best chance of survival. His actions are always rationalised in terms of saving lives; the executions are shown to have had the desired effect as he discovers the Japanese plans for a counter-attack as a result. Bearded sweaty and dishevelled, his often manic performance goes against traditional heroism, although he does die the classic hero's death trying to defy the enemy to the last. However, at the end of the film there is no real sense of moral superiority in a characterisation which remains highly ambivalent.

Hell is a City is in many respects a formulaic police drama. Baker plays the hard-bitten Inspector Martineau who is investigating a hold-up while also tracking down an escaped gangster who has a grudge against him. It employs almost exactly the same crew as *Yesterday's Enemy*, including experienced director Val Guest (who also wrote the screenplay), with Michael Carreras, son of Hammer's chief executive James Carreras, in charge of the production. This time, however, with the major company ABPC involved as distributor, the film has a glossier finish. Some sequences opt for New Wave style realism, making the best of location work in Manchester. The most striking of these is the illegal gambling sequence starkly photographed on an area of wasteland. Otherwise, with its fast pace, terse dialogue, and the casting of American John Crawford as the villain (Don Starling), the film follows the model for crime films established by Hollywood. In typical fashion, Hammer went for the jugular in their advertising campaign playing heavily on contemporary anxieties about rising levels of street crime. The main poster is captioned 'Violence in the street', while their press book offers audiences the warning 'This could be your city – today! Get out of the city . . . where hell threatens to break loose – any moment now!' One noticeable aspect of the advertising is that Baker is not just the star of the film but that he appears to be carrying it. For the first time in his career, his is the name above the title.

Martineau's tough-guy ethics are established in two scenes. He is bullying and aggressive when he interrogates Chloe Hawkins, played by a young Billie Whitelaw, threatening to reveal her adultery to her husband if she doesn't provide him with the information he needs. Similarly, when questioning another member of Starling's gang, he threatens to frame the man's innocent brother if he doesn't confess his part in the robbery. At the same time, vulnerability is established through the depiction of his troubled relationship with his wife (Maxine Audley). She feels neglected because of the long hours he spends at work, while he is frustrated by her unwillingness to start a family. His code of morality is clear enough: he even saves Starling from death when he nearly falls from a rooftop while Martineau is apprehending him, but there is an element of self-doubt; he is visibly troubled by the subsequent execution of Starling, commenting 'none of us is perfect'. It is interesting to note that the film's original ending had him resolving his differences with his wife before a discreet fade leaves them together in their bedroom. In the released version, Martineau is left wandering the streets, a lonely figure, still pondering the possibility of an illicit affair which has been offered him by the barmaid 'Lucky'. A press release from the film's American distributor, Warner, plays up Baker's new persona:

> He is a believably virile man, who is building himself a personality that is unique in British pictures: tough, down to earth, very masculine, but capable of tenderness at the right moment. This almost Bogart-like he-man provides a refreshing change from the rather neurotic, mixed-up heroes who have been in fashion for a while now.

Only the last sentence doesn't ring true, as Martineau is actually a remarkably confused, uncertain character. His moral uncertainty is indicated by his odd affinity with Starling when he confesses: 'I know how his mind works. I grew up with him. We went to the same school, fought in the same war.' Andrew Spicer goes as far as to suggest that Starling is Martineau's doppelgänger, a sort of distorted mirror image: they use similar methods, but for different ends.

The film was well received: it was nominated for two BAFTAs – *Yesterday's Enemy* picked up four nominations. Baker had some of the strongest notices of his career. The *Daily Mail* was particularly enthusiastic: 'A splendid performance this. Mr Baker has the ability to infect any film in which he appears with his own quality of restless, controlled fury. Like a grenade with the pin half pulled out.' Derek Monsey in the *Sunday Express* said 'Stanley Baker is as bleak and tough as only Stanley Baker can be', while the *Star* proclaimed that Baker 'is easily the best copper in the celluloid film force'. The review in the *Daily Herald* summarised the cumulative impact that Baker was having in his recent films: 'He is so utterly against the run of leading men. His big boxer's body, crag of a chin, his flat voice and assertive masculinity all make him the odd man out of British films.' There seemed to be a recognition that Baker had created a new form of star type for British cinema, one which was striking a chord with contemporary audiences. Warner's press release for *Hell is a City* reflected this when it claimed 'suddenly, it seems, everyone wants Stanley Baker. Today he is Britain's hottest box-office proposition – an actor who can be relied on to give a first rate performance *and* one of the few to bring in the

public.' Leaving aside the studio hyperbole, there is a genuine acknow-
ledgement here of the impact Baker had made on recent British films. He
represented something different; a new kind of hero for the start of a very
different era.

CHAPTER FOUR

The Hero of Rorke's Drift

Between 1950 and 1964 (when his most famous film, *Zulu*, was released) Stanley Baker's life and career had undergone an astonishing change. At the start of the 1950s he was a young man of twenty-one, a struggling, frequently out of work actor, living alone in London. By the mid 1960s he was one of the most popular and highest paid actors working in British cinema (Anthony Storey records that at his height he commanded £120,000 per picture). Married now for nearly fifteen years, he was living with his family in considerable comfort in Wimbledon. By the middle of the previous decade he was already in regular employment as a supporting actor, even if frequently typecast as the villain, and under contract to the indulgent Alexander Korda. By the end of the 1950s he had moved from Korda to Rank and then into contractual independence, had achieved a degree of stardom and recast his public image to become the best recognised tough guy in British films. By 1960 he was already the veteran of over thirty feature films, as well as having appeared in the theatre and on television. Entering the new decade, his status within the domestic industry was high and soon to go higher. While this rise was largely due to his own drive and single-mindedness, there is little doubt that he benefited from the changes taking place around him in wider society, as well as in the indigenous film industry. The new image that he offered to audiences, as a working-class hero with scant respect for authority, chimed perfectly with a transformation that was taking place in Britain itself.

The most obvious change was politically, with the return of a Labour government in 1964 (albeit with a tiny majority). With this a dozen years of Tory rule were brought to an end. The final years of Conservative prime ministers Macmillan and Douglas-Home were dogged with scandals, most notably the Profumo affair. The mood of deference towards those in power which marked the 1950s was quickly gone and the declining Tory administration was lampooned by the wits of the satire boom, typified by the television programme *That Was The Week That Was* and the newly launched magazine *Private Eye*. Young people were in rebellion too. With the end of National Service and an abundance of employment, the young had money to spend and plenty to spend it on, with an explosion in popular music, magazines and groundbreaking fashions. Television had brought the outside world closer, reflected in a growing interest in imported foreign ideas, whether it was existentialist philosophy or rock and roll. Other notions about personal freedom and equality were filtering in from America where the civil rights movement was having an enormous impact. Class barriers in Britain were crumbling as the media began to focus increasingly on the proletarian heroes that were bringing fresh talent into music, literature, sport and the cinema. There was an air of accelerating change about the country as the certainties of the immediate postwar era seemed to be swept away and Britain raced into the colourful, exuberant optimism of the Swinging Sixties.

British cinema was quick to pick up on these developments. There was a new audience to appeal to and one that was increasingly dominated by the affluent, urban young. The first signs of change had come with the films of the New Wave, celebrations of working-class culture which drew heavily on the 'angry young man' phenomenon in the theatre and literature of the late 1950s. These new films, including *Room at the Top* (1959) and *Saturday Night and Sunday Morning* (1960), were dubbed by the press as 'kitchen sink' films, but they appealed to a public that had never before seen working-class life represented with such authenticity. The rebellious nature of characters like Arthur Seaton (Albert Finney), sticking two fingers up at authority and out for a good time, was a world away from the gentlemanly politeness of 1950s stars like Kenneth More and Richard Todd. By the early 1960s these films had served their purpose; their unrelenting grimness was quickly out of tune with the joyful hedonism sweeping the country's youth. The change couldn't be better illustrated than in the big cinematic hit of 1963, Tony Richardson's *Tom Jones*. Here Finney was transformed from the sullen, ill-tempered Arthur Seaton. Now he was a smiling rogue, chasing wine, women and song across a merry England that seemed more than ready to indulge him. The film struck a nerve with the public, capturing the mood of a country on the edge of profound and controversial change.

Hollywood wasn't slow to recognise that British cinema was undergoing a resurgence. The international success of *Tom Jones* and the first two Bond films – *Dr No* (1962) and *From Russia With Love* (1963) – hadn't gone unnoticed, particularly as all three films had been bankrolled by the London offices of United Artists. There was money to be made in Britain and most Hollywood production companies sought to cash in on this during the decade. The effects of an influx of American finance into British cinema are apparent in three films which Stanley Baker appeared in between 1959 and 1962. The first of these was *The Angry Hills* (1959), a product of MGM's

London set-up put together by producer Raymond Stross. Set in occupied Greece during the Second World War, it follows the adventures of an American war correspondent, played by Hollywood star Robert Mitchum, who obtains the names of Nazi collaborators and then flees across Greece aided by the resistance and pursued by the Germans. The film was adapted from the novel by Leon Uris and directed by the dynamic American Robert Aldrich. As was common with American projects filmed in Europe, the supporting cast was made up with native character actors like Marius Goring and Donald Wolfit. It also benefited from the work of future Bond movies designer Ken Adam and cinematographer Stephen Dade (who was to be director of photography on *Zulu*). Dade's strikingly atmospheric photography, especially for the location work in Greece, remains the most arresting feature of an otherwise overly talkative and predictable action-adventure yarn. The film marked the beginning of a friendship between Baker and Mitchum, but the American star seems uninvolved here and ambles through the film in the nonchalant manner that was to become a trademark. Although it was flattering enough for Baker to be cast in an ambitious, Hollywood-backed production with second billing to an international star of Mitchum's calibre, he was inevitably relegated to playing the villain again, this time the Nazi agent Conrad Heisler. Aldrich's attempts to use the film to explore moral questions, as he had done with his successful war melodrama *Attack* (1956), don't really work here and MGM cut the film by fifteen minutes for its American release.

Aldrich joined the growing list of American filmmakers who appreciated Baker's qualities as a performer and wanted to work with him. The first product of this was the offer to appear in a planned twenty-eight episode series for American television about an Englishman living in New York. The press reported that Baker had been offered half a million pounds to take the lead but he turned it down, telling *Photoplay*: 'I'm not particularly interested in spending two years in Hollywood, which will mean uprooting my family . . . I love Britain. I want to make pictures in this country, about this country.' Baker did, however, work with Aldrich again on the ill-fated biblical epic *Sodom and Gomorrah* (1962). The film proved to be a prime example of the hazards which can beset international co-productions, with so many hands involved that chaos descends. Shot in both English- and Italian-language versions, with responsibility for the production split between an Italian company (Titanus) and a French studio (Pathé), with Rank picking up the British release and independent producer Joseph E. Levine looking after the American end of things, it had disaster written all over it; Levine was eventually to be a crucial figure in the making of *Zulu*, as well as in Baker's career in the late 1960s. Aldrich's assistant responsible for completion of the Italian language version of the film was Sergio Leone, the future director of spaghetti westerns. The film's melting pot of nationalities extended to the cast which includes English actor Stewart Granger as Lot, the Italians Pier Angeli and Rossana Podestà playing his wife and daughter respectively, and the French actress Anouk Aimée as the queen of Sodom and Gomorrah.

The film is a wearying combination of slow-paced solemnity and the occasional bout of sensationalist violence. The emphasis on the lurid possibilities of the story was signalled to audiences by the racy advertising campaign which promised sex and brutality galore. With censorship as it was in 1962, the possibility of real sexual explicitness was a hollow claim and the film is a tease in this respect, as indicated by the opening sequence where we see the aftermath of an orgy with the participants lying around exhausted, and a lascivious-looking Baker leering into the camera with a smug expression. The censor was more tolerant about the violence, so we are treated to impaling and slaves being burnt alive. Aldrich wasn't renowned for his subtlety and he certainly takes a blunt approach to the subject, taking a perverse glee in the sadistic sequences, which rather undermines the film's high moral tone. We even have suggestions of incest in the relationship between the queen and her brother, Astaroth, played by Baker. As ever, Baker acquits himself well within the limitations of the role, managing to convey a sense of underlying evil and barely suppressed menace. However, he is given such a lipsmackingly nasty part (the crowning glory of which is taking the virginity of both of Lot's daughters) that he has difficulty avoiding unintentional humour. The possibilities of international co-productions were considerable, but *Sodom and Gomorrah* is a textbook example of what can go wrong.

If both *The Angry Hills* and *Sodom and Gomorrah* returned Baker to the villainy of his earlier film roles, his third international film of this period indicated more securely his new status and the opportunities it could bring. *The Guns of Navarone* (1961), adapted from Alistair MacLean's novel, remains one of the most popular films Baker was to appear in and helped to pave the way for *Zulu*. The film was the brainchild of the American producer/writer Carl Foreman, another victim of the McCarthy witch-hunts, who was attempting to re-establish his reputation in the liberal climate of the 1960s. The first-choice director Alexander Mackendrick was replaced, apparently due to his overly fussy approach to the action sequences, by the more easy-going, robust J. Lee Thompson who had proved he could handle genre material of this kind with *Ice Cold in Alex* (1958). Studio work was completed at Shepperton and the spectacular location shooting was mainly filmed on the Greek island of Rhodes. Baker appears to have had a great deal of fun making the film. Promotional footage shows the cast enjoying visits to the set by the Greek prime minister, the former royal family of Romania, and the king and queen of Greece. The cast are seen entertaining themselves with an ongoing chess tournament, with Anthony Quinn proving to be the champion. Quinn and Baker became friends forming an 'opposing camp' to the friendship formed by Gregory Peck and David Niven, who seemingly didn't entirely approve of the boisterous behaviour of Baker and Quinn. Baker later told Clive James: 'We had a great time. Just working on that film was worth it for meeting Anthony Quinn because he's a great character. He's a marvellous guy, a lovely actor – flamboyant, over-acts a great deal of the time, but it doesn't matter because he loves it.'

The film was an enormous production employing the Greek army and navy, with a huge set built at Shepperton, as well as three scale models ready for destruction. The total production cost was $6 million, making it Columbia Pictures' most expensive film to date. For Baker, there was fourth billing behind his glamorous Hollywood co-stars, a fact acknowledged in the film's trailer where he is named (this had not been the case in his American-backed films of the early 1950s). His association with films aimed at the American market had paid off with a degree of recognition in the States which few British stars had at this time, although Columbia's promotional campaign for the film included posters which firmly reinforce his position in the second rank of stardom behind the likes of Peck and Niven.

The film opened with the full fanfare reserved for a studio blockbuster, complete with a world premiere in London attended by the Queen and Prince Philip. It garnered seven Oscar nominations (winning one for its special effects) and was the top-grossing film of 1961.

Baker's role is in the line of his sympathetic tough guys, rather than the villainous parts that Hollywood had more usually bestowed on him. Columbia's press materials emphasised this with a piece headed 'Heavy with a heart.' Baker's character, 'Butcher' Brown, the man assigned as the driver/engineer for the assault on Navarone, is first introduced with a description provided by Commodore Jensen (James Robertson Justice). He explains that Brown is a dab hand with a knife and served with the Republicans during the Spanish Civil War, picking up his nickname of the 'butcher of Barcelona'. Immediately Baker's tough-guy credentials are confirmed when we first see him looking sullen, closely inspecting his knife. However, we quickly discover his vulnerable, troubled side when he hesitates in killing a German sailor, later informing Gregory Peck's Captain Mallory that he has had enough killing at close quarters and has made his own personal peace treaty with the enemy. His questioning attitude and inner turmoil add the element of ambiguity which was becoming so important to Baker's screen persona. His rejection of violence later costs him his own life when another hesitation results in him being stabbed with his own knife. Baker's character is one of several narrative methods used by Carl Foreman to explore the ethical questions raised by war, although these are less the film's focus than the stirringly staged 'Boy's Own' heroics. Either way, Baker is afforded a role which is both heroic and sympathetic, in a major international success whose appeal has continued over the years.

The popularity of *The Guns of Navarone* could easily have led to a career in Hollywood, but this appears to be something that Baker consciously rejected. Ellen confirms that there were offers of contracts and work in America but that Stanley wasn't tempted to follow his friend Richard Burton across the Atlantic. As he jokingly put it himself, America already had one Robert Mitchum and he couldn't see why it would need another. Ellen attributes his attitude to two things: first, his genuine commitment to filmmaking in Britain; and secondly his need to be close to his homeland, Wales. Neither of these factors should be underestimated. His concern with the state of his native film industry was to become an important factor in the direction his career took in the 1960s and his love for Wales was never in doubt. His sister, Muriel, suggests that he always hankered for Wales and could never forget his childhood. She recounts stories of his regular visits home to Ferndale where he would go out with 'the lads', always making sure there was plenty of money behind the bar for drinks all round. She remembered one occasion when he was asked by a man to autograph his shirt sleeve but refused, pointing out that his wife wouldn't be too happy about having to wash it; he signed a card for him instead. Visits home grounded him in a sense of his own identity. In his memoir of Baker, Anthony Storey recounts a conversation in which Stanley questioned whether he should ever have left Wales at all. It's evident that there was only one reason for doing this; that he *had* to go if he wanted to be an actor – he had to go where the work was. At the same time, there is still a tone of regret as he ruminates over the fact that he is now living in England and Spain, with his children at school in England. As he admitted, his heart always remained in Wales.

Those feelings were to find their expression in the film which he referred to as his Welsh western, *Zulu*. The origins of the film lay in an article published in *Lilliput* magazine in April 1958 entitled 'Slaughter in the sun' and credited to John Curtis, the pen name of writer John Prebble. The article was part of a series called 'Stories of endurance' which focused on heroic tales about recipients of the Victoria Cross, the highest British military decoration. The events at Rorke's Drift in South Africa provided Prebble with ideal material, being the story of a single battle for which the greatest number of Victoria Crosses, ten in all, had been awarded. Prebble was initially approached about the possibility of a television adaptation of his article. This came to nothing, but through it he met the director Cy Endfield and was then commissioned to begin work on a film script. Even by normal production standards, the gestation period for what eventually became *Zulu* was unusually long. Prebble later told BBC Wales producer Steve Freer about the initial reasons for Endfield's difficulties in taking the script into production: 'He had no money, and I think I was paid two hundred quid in the hope of making more should it ever get on the screen. And about a year after that Stanley came into it.' Baker and Endfield were by this time close friends, having already worked together on four films. It was therefore understandable that Endfield should show Baker his plans and notes for the film, but Baker seems to have been attracted to the project by one particular aspect of the script: its Welsh dimension. As Sheldon Hall points out in his meticulous study of the film, the 24th Regiment of Foot was actually an English unit who happened to have a recruiting office in the Welsh town of Brecon and, therefore, a slightly larger number of Welsh recruits in their ranks than might normally be the case. Only at a later date, *after* the battle at Rorke's Drift, were they to become a fully fledged Welsh regiment, the South Wales Borderers. Not that this deterred Baker; he could see the possibility of making a film which might pay affectionate tribute to his homeland and the heroism of its native sons. As Prebble put it himself, 'Wales prevailed everywhere when Stanley was working'. When the film was eventually made, the 24th Regiment of Foot had magically become the South Wales Borderers.

As previously recounted, Endfield had first worked with Baker on the modest family drama *A Child in the House* (1956). However their second collaboration resulted in *Hell Drivers* (1957), which played such a crucial role in changing Baker's screen persona. Cyril Raker Endfield was born in Scranton, Pennsylvania in 1914 and studied at Yale, although he never graduated. During the 1930s he worked in a number of liberal theatre projects which developed as part of President Roosevelt's progressive New Deal policies. While a student, Endfield had already developed his political interests and briefly became involved with the Young Communist League. However, his radicalism seems to have been more the expression of a natural sympathy for the underprivileged and disenfranchised rather than a hard-line concern with party politics. In contrast, another of his abiding passions was for magic, especially card tricks. It was this that, according to legend, led him to gain entry to Orson Welles's Mercury production company in Hollywood in the early 1940s after the great filmmaker had been impressed by his talent for conjuring. For the next ten years he worked regularly as a director, making eight short films and seven features. The majority of his feature films were routine, low cost B-movies like *Tarzan's Savage Fury* (1952), but his liberal inclinations were given voice in the lynch mob drama *The Sound of Fury* (1950) and the taut thriller *The Underworld Story* (1950). His first short film, *Inflation* (1942), had been shelved after complaints from the American Chamber of Commerce that it was anti-capitalist. In 1951 he fled the United States after coming under investigation by the House Un-American Activities Committee (HUAC) and resettled in Britain. Here he worked in television for ITV before graduating to a number of B-movies, writing and directing under a series of pseudonyms including C. Raker Endfield and Hugh Raker so as to avoid any problems with American distributors.

Following *Hell Drivers*, Baker and Endfield made two further films together. The first was *Sea Fury* (1958), made while Stanley was still under contract to Rank. This is an undemanding seafaring adventure set off the coast of Spain, with the American actor Victor McLaglen making his last screen appearance as an ageing tugboat captain. Baker is a crew member who clashes with the captain over the woman they are both in love with. The cast also features the young actors Robert Shaw and Barry Foster. The only highlight is the climactic storm sequence which is handled with Endfield's customary vigour, as Baker struggles manfully in the flooded hold of a sinking freighter, trying to manhandle a drum of dangerous sodium over the side. Baker's physical stature at least makes him convincing in these scenes. Unfortunately, the laboured romantic subplot drags the whole enterprise to the bottom of the sea. The next film on which Baker and Endfield collaborated was *Jet Storm* (1959), made after Stanley had walked out of his Rank contract. It was shot for Endfield's own Pendennis production outfit, with the backing of British Lion. Baker is the pilot of an aircraft which a crazed bomber (Richard Attenborough) tries to blow up. The film develops along the lines of a soap opera, or perhaps a forerunner of the disaster movies of the 1970s, with an all-star cast (Diane Cilento, Mai Zetterling, pop star Marty Wilde, Elizabeth Sellers and Harry Secombe) acting out a series of small dramas while the main narrative ticks over in the background. Endfield and Baker handle both films efficiently, but they made little impact at the box office and didn't extend the range of either director or star. Nonetheless, by the time they began to work together on *Zulu* they had completed four films together and formed a sympathetic team.

The process of getting *Zulu* off the ground proved to be an arduous one which was to take five years in all. During this period Endfield continued his career by working in advertising, television and the theatre, enjoying considerable success with the West End run of Neil Simon's first play *Come Blow Your Horn*. While staging the play he held casting sessions for *Zulu* in the theatre's bar. Baker also continued to be in regular employment, making three more films in the eighteen months leading up to the shoot for *Zulu*. The first was an effective caper film called *A Prize of Arms* (1962), which owes something to Dearden and Relph's earlier *The League of Gentlemen* (1960), as well as being a precursor for Baker's later crime movie *Robbery* (1967). The film is distinctive for casting Baker in an anti-hero role as a likeable criminal. He is a disillusioned, cynical ex-army officer who, along with another pal from service days (an explosives expert played by Helmut Schmid) and a nervy youth fresh from National Service (Tom Bell), plans the theft of a payroll from an army camp. Derived from an original story by future director Nicholas Roeg, the film is briskly entertaining with the focus on the detailed planning and execution of the job. Only the heavily moralistic ending which censorship insisted on mars the neatly worked out logic of the robbery. The film manages to be smartly topical in both style and subject matter. The visual approach borrows from the realism of the New Wave in its sense of place and gritty look, while there is a mood of rebellion in the disenchantment of Baker's character who has been drifting aimlessly since the end of the war: 'If you want anything in this world you've just got to go out and take it.' The robbery itself takes place against the background of an unspecified military engagement overseas, which has obvious echoes of the Suez Crisis of six years earlier. Baker's role gives him another opportunity to blur moral boundaries, with the audience firmly on his side, willing him on to succeed.

In the French Style (1963) was an American–French co-production funded by Columbia Pictures and designed as a vehicle for the emerging star Jean Seberg. Adapted from his own novel by Irwin Shaw and directed by the American Robert Parrish, it is a glossy, superficially risqué romantic drama with Baker playing one of the many lovers of an American art student in Paris. The cinematography makes the most of the locations, but Baker has little chance to register in a film which places its hauntingly glamorous female star so firmly as the centre of interest. It at least confirmed that Baker could play romantic roles and, as Ellen Baker confirms, was a project that Baker enjoyed working on. The last, and possibly least, of the films he made before embarking on filming *Zulu* was *The Man Who Finally Died* (1963), like *A Prize of Arms* made cheaply by a small independent production company under the auspices of British Lion. Adapted from a popular television series written by Lewis Greifer, it is a complex spy thriller shot partly on location in Bavaria. Baker, looking decidedly American in dark sunglasses, is the German-born Englishman who tries to unravel the mystery of his father's death, uncovering what initially appears to be an insurance scam, but which is subsequently revealed to be a Cold War struggle between East and West for possession of a rocket scientist. Baker is typically intense, and is provided with an array of terse one-liners, but the story is flatly handled, suffers from an unconvincing romantic subplot, and is too flimsy to support some high-minded statements about the pointlessness of Cold War politics. It did, however, team Baker with a number of the personnel who he would work with again on *Zulu*, from cinematographer Stephen Dade and assistant director Bob Porter, to actor Nigel Green, who was to be so memorable as Colour Sergeant Bourne.

One of Baker's more interesting projects in the period when *Zulu* was in preparation was a television production for BBC Wales called *The Squeeze* (1960). Shot at their Cardiff studios and screened nationally as part of the *Sunday Night Play* slot, it provided Stanley with an all too rare opportunity to be involved in a Welsh subject. It was also a reflection of growing status that his fee of £1,000 was then the highest that BBC Wales had ever paid to an actor. The role allowed him to play the part of a miner and to speak with his native accent. Although technically dated (the story largely takes place in two rooms of the family house, with restricted camera movement and little cutting, rather like a filmed stage play), the drama is interesting for its examination of the psychology of Welsh working-class masculinity. Harry Green's script is vaguely reminiscent of D. H. Lawrence in its unpicking of the motivations of Baker's character, 'Big Tom'. Tom is persuaded by his wife to give up working underground but consequently suffers a crisis of identity which drives him to a brief fling with the pit's nurse. His sense of his own masculinity is intrinsically bound up with working at the coalface and with the position this gives him in the community. He finally returns to his old job with a feeling of satisfaction. Although the dialogue is occasionally stilted, the drama deals with its subject in a serious, thoughtful manner and provided Baker with a part which demonstrated his physical presence and his intensity as a performer. The nuances of the characterisation prefigure some of his best work with Joseph Losey.

Zulu was to be significant for Baker in a number of ways, not least as it took him behind the camera and into production for the first time. It was a logical move for a man who was increasingly trying to take control of his own career. As early as 1960 he had formed Stanley Baker Arts, partly for tax purposes, but also to allow him to try to develop projects of his own. To make *Zulu* he set up the production company Diamond Films and went into a more concrete partnership with Endfield, with the two of them acting as co-producers. The subject, with its Welsh dimension, provided Baker with the perfect project to make his debut as a producer, one with which he could feel personally involved. He wasn't the first British actor to branch out in this way; Richard Attenborough, Bryan Forbes and Jack Hawkins had already joined forces to form the Allied Filmmakers consortium, but the scale of Baker's ambition with a production like *Zulu* was considerable. Not least among the difficulties he faced, and the principle reason for delay, was the problem of raising the finance he needed. He had been rejected by every production company he approached in Britain, where he was clearly seen as an actor who was getting out of his depth. The answer came in the form of maverick American producer Joseph E. Levine, who Baker had met during the making of *Sodom and Gomorrah*. As Sheldon Hall points out, the story of how Baker persuaded Levine to back *Zulu* became a regular party piece over the years, becoming more embroidered with each retelling. Boiled down to its essence, Levine was a shrewd, instinctive businessman who seems to have genuinely liked Stanley. When Baker took him up on an earlier offer to back a project of his, if Baker could come up with one, Levine was as good as his word. The commercial appeal of the film was Levine's principle interest and he was willing to put his faith in his first-time producer with the shake of a hand, impressed by his drive and commitment.

Levine and his production company, Embassy, had a track record of producing and distributing successful costume adventure films shot in Europe. He had developed links with the major Hollywood producer Paramount who saw him as someone who could bring them highly commercial properties, and manage those projects with flair and efficiency. His strength lay in the ability to aggressively market his films. He persuaded Paramount to back *Zulu* with a budget of around $2 million. He would handle publicity and promotion for the film on its completion. Baker and Endfield were left with the job of actually getting the film made for a budget that was substantially lower than their original estimate. Necessity proved to be the mother of invention and they were able to reduce costs by manufacturing most of their costumes, props and sets in-house rather than buying them from expensive suppliers in London. With a budget which only provided four hundred Zulu extras when they needed to give the impression of ten times that number, the props department came up with an ingenious solution. For the magnificent long shots in which we see the Zulus spread out against the skyline, shields were nailed on to long poles and held horizontally between two Zulu warriors giving the appearance of ten men instead of two. As second unit director Bob Porter pointed out, if you look closely enough you can see that the warriors don't have any legs. To further save money the hospital block scenes were shot in the studios at Twicken-ham rather than on location, so that actor James Booth (playing the part of Private Hook) never actually set foot in South Africa. When the location shoot was delayed by two weeks of bad weather, the time was utilised by Endfield and Baker to drill the cast and crew so that when the weather finally broke they could shoot at greater speed. Ellen recalled that within the first month of filming they had made up all the time that had been lost. Among the many unusual production difficulties which Baker encountered was an invasion by baboons who took a liking to the encampment set and couldn't be shifted from their new home. The film was eventually brought in under budget and looked spectacular, despite the prudence with which it had been made.

As well as requiring almost military efficiency to organise, the location shooting in South Africa required Baker to utilise his diplomatic skills. The Zulus had never seen a film, let alone experienced making one, so Baker had some silent movies shipped in and arranged screenings of Buster Keaton and Laurel and Hardy to introduce them to the magic of cinema. They seem to have quickly entered into the spirit of things and particularly enjoyed taking part in the battle sequences. If some of the anecdotes which have appeared about working with the Zulus come a little close to condescension, it seems to be true that Baker had to be inventive to counter the attitudes of the South African authorities who would not allow the Zulus to be paid at anything like the normal rate. Consequently, he allowed them to help themselves to the props and other materials used in the production, including the cattle, as soon as the filming was complete. A genuine bond of affection and respect developed between the cast and crew and the Zulus during the production, with Baker himself deeply affected by the experi-ence. When Baker died, the Zulu leader Chief Buthelezi (who appears in the film playing Cetewayo) sent a wreath for his funeral with a tribute describing Baker as the finest white man he had met. In a final, awful irony, *Zulu* was designated by the South African censors as 'unfit for black consumption' and could not be seen by the Zulus who had acted in it. The censors seem to have been especially sensitive to a film which depicted the fighting prowess of black South Africans. When he found out about the ban, Baker arranged a special screening for those who had taken part in the film.

A more serious level of difficulty arose from shooting under the strictures of South Africa's policy of apartheid. As Sheldon Hall describes it, the cast and crew were decidedly innocent when it came to appreciating exactly what apartheid meant in practice. With police and security forces in close attendance, Baker was forced to maintain tight control over the location, ensuring that fraternisation between white and black members of the team were kept to a minimum for their own protection. As an avowed liberal, it was an uncomfortable experience but the consequences of breaching South Africa's laws were made obvious to everyone by the authorities. Baker had a job to complete, to get the film made without any serious incident, and set about this in a characteristically pragmatic manner. Nonetheless, everything was done to minimise the effects of the apartheid regulations on those taking part in the shoot itself, but this was a process of constant negotiation. A story told by Michael Caine in his autobiography captures the tension of the situation:

> One day I saw a black worker make a mistake and I stopped to watch him getting a real telling off. To my astonishment, the foreman didn't reprimand him; he smashed a fist into his face instead. I was so shocked at this I couldn't move and then suddenly I started to run towards the man, screaming at him, but Stanley got there first. I had never seen him so angry. He fired the man on the spot and then gathered all the white gang bosses together and laid down the law on how everyone was going to be treated on this film set from then on. It brought home for the first time what this word 'apartheid' really meant.

From a contemporary perspective we might question the whole undertaking of filming in apartheid South Africa, but at the time no boycott existed and a degree of expediency seems to have ruled the day. In the circumstances, Baker and the rest of his team seem to have done what they could within the confines of the situation to ensure that things proceeded in as civilised a manner as possible; inevitably this meant a degree of compromise with the apartheid system.

A specific instance of this occurred when the South African State Department of Information decided it wanted to film a behind the scenes documentary about the making of *Zulu*. Their intention seems to have been to make a propaganda piece to extol the virtues of the apartheid regime, showing how people of different races could actually work together on a project of this kind. Baker appears to have begrudgingly conceded (he probably had very little choice) but made sure that he appeared in the footage as little as possible. In the end, the film seems never to have been released. In a bizarre coda to this story, cans of raw black and white footage from the film eventually turned up in a saleroom in Southampton and were purchased by a Dutch-born doctor, Jay Pinto, a collector of 16 mm prints and other film memorabilia. A selection from the twenty-six minutes of footage will hopefully be appearing in a new DVD special edition of *Zulu*.

Baker appears both to have excelled in his new role as producer and to have genuinely enjoyed the experience. Bob Porter recalls Baker as being determined and professional during the shoot, with a grasp for detail and organisation. He was also patient and generous, particularly towards his fellow actors. He established a reputation for running a tight ship, including being scrupulously honest in his business transactions. Actor Glynn Edwards, who played Corporal Allen, remembered that although Baker liked to enjoy himself as soon as the day's filming was done, he was completely focused when they were filming. Baker immersed himself in the specifics of the task but also seems to have relished the degree to which the project appealed to the risk taker in him. In an interview with *Photoplay* headlined 'Stanley Baker: soft-hearted gambler' he says: 'It was a fantastic gamble, the whole thing, but I never had any doubt about its eventual success.' The film also demonstrated the depth of his self-belief. It was the culmination of an interest in the mechanics of filmmaking which had begun when he first worked with Joseph Losey. Ellen confirms that it was Losey who first showed an interest in discussing methods of filmmaking with Baker and who began to whet his appetite for being more involved behind the camera. Baker explained to Clive James: 'It all stemmed originally from the involvement that Losey made me aware of and I thought there's a better and a bigger thing to do than just acting in a film and that is to make films.' For Ellen it was a mixed experience, as the man she had married was changing before her eyes. As she told a number of interviewers, she had happily married a fellow actor but had not expected to find herself wedded to a producer, with all the considerable strains and pressures this entailed. Despite this, it quickly became evident that Baker had found a new forte which would shape his subsequent career.

With the completion of shooting and post-production back in Britain, there was now the job of selling the film to the public. A good deal of the subsequent publicity centred on the scale of the production itself. *Film Review* magazine, the in-house publication of the ABC cinema chain, described it as a film 'planned on an epic scale' with major construction work required to dam the Tugela River and the building of a complete replica of the encampment at Rorke's Drift, 'including a hospital, a church, a store, a stable and cattle kraal'. Another element in the promotional campaign was the decision to lay emphasis on the patriotic appeal of the story, particularly the awarding of ten Victoria Crosses. Paramount's press book advised cinema managers to arrange displays which would draw attention to this. The thunderous posters for the film proclaimed that it would be 'Dwarfing the Mightiest! Towering over the Greatest!' with the word 'Zulu' spelt out in enormous lettering. Possibly the most bizarre aspect of the campaign was the release of a pop single written by the film's composer John Barry, which attempted to create a new dance craze called the 'Zulu Stamp'. The record came complete with a guide to the dance steps.

It is interesting to note that promotional materials used for subsequent reissues on video and DVD have gradually excised Baker from the film and instead placed the emphasis on Michael Caine. On the otherwise excellent Paramount DVD of the film, it is Caine whose name appears above the title and Baker is nowhere to be seen on the cover.

Seeing the film today, Baker has clearly been successful in drawing out the story's potential for celebrating Welshness. Apart from the fact that the regiment appears to be almost entirely made up of Welsh soldiers (there are so many Joneses that they have to be identified by their numbers), there are several direct references to remind the audience of the fact. The men frequently sing to keep up their spirits and Ivor Emmanuel's character seems more interested in protecting the various members of the regimental choir than in the outcome of the battle. Private Thomas, played by Neil McCarthy, is seen tending a calf which is eventually killed during the battle. He bemoans the fact that the land in Natal Province is so poor: 'This country is not as good as Bala.' The culmination of this element in the film is undoubtedly the singing of 'Men of Harlech' as a response to the chanting of the Zulus. Baker turns to Emmanuel and exhorts him: 'Do you think the Welsh can't do better than that?' Just to reinforce the Welsh dimension, the singing of 'Men of Harlech' was recorded on a hillside near Ferndale with the members of local male voice choir under the direction of Ivor Emmanuel. The scene evokes a great sense of Welsh pride and must have reminded Baker of his regular visits to Cardiff Arms Park to watch his beloved Welsh rugby team and hear the passionate singing of the crowd. As Peter Stead puts it, 'there was no need for embarrassment here for this was a movie that almost every Welsh filmgoer would want on a desert island'.

Baker had maintained his links to Wales, although it was always a matter of instinctive feeling rather than any conscious plan. A number of people in Ferndale have memories of him coming back home on a regular basis. Ellen confirms that in his mind Ferndale was, and remained, his home. Alwyn Jones remembers that there was 'never any side' to Stanley and that when he was back in Ferndale he easily slipped into the community again without undue fuss. His cousin Joan Howells recalls everyone in the village being immensely proud of him and the fact that he remained 'down to earth'. Striving for success was a Rhondda characteristic possessed by more than just Stanley; he was one among a number of local heroes produced by the valleys. Barry Sullivan recalled the succession of gleaming cars in which Stanley would roll up, including on one occasion a Zephyr Zodiac with the then unheard-of luxury of a radio inside. What is striking, in an area which was all too used to suffering unemployment and poverty, was the lack of resentment towards Baker's success and wealth. Rather there is collective pride in someone who had made something of himself and therefore reflected his community positively. Back in Ferndale the mantle of the film star could be relaxed and he could be his natural self. David Williams recalls how one afternoon he was helping a friend to mend his garden fence in Albany Street and hurt his hand in the process. To his amazement, the neighbour who popped out to help, bringing him a cup of tea, was Stanley Baker, home visiting his mother. For Baker, maintaining his connection to Ferndale was part of keeping his own sense of identity.

The fact that he remained a working-class Welshman at heart was also a key part of his public persona. An article in the *Sunday Express* entitled 'How I hate flattery grumbles Mr Baker' suggests that for all his success he manages to keep his feet on the ground. Asked if he feels the sense of alienation from his roots which other working-class stars like Albert Finney had confessed to, he replies:

> Not at all. I'm happiest when I'm working, but I also know who I am in real life. I'm the son of a Welsh coal miner. From the age of thirteen I have been an actor. I've been married for fourteen years to a wife I love. I'm the father of four children. That's who I am. A working-class background can give you great security. You remember what life was like. You appreciate that your life is better now – and it's you who've made it so. That gives you confidence – and a sense of values.

An article in *Photoplay* opens by informing us that Baker has 'a lavish home in Wimbledon, situated in an acre or two of grounds complete with swimming pool, a Bentley, a Jaguar – yet somehow, you get the impression that much as he enjoys the fruits of success, they are almost completely unimportant to him'. Another article from the early 1960s finds him holidaying in the Lebanon, playing the local casino and telling the reporter: 'I'm here because I believe in enjoying my money! I have no guilt complex about it like some people. I earned it and I like spending it.' But there is no real contradiction here between the rich film star and the working-class boy from the Rhondda. In keeping with the image, Baker enjoys the rewards of his labour just like any member of the public would do in his place. But he doesn't forget where he came from or how it felt to have very little. In cultivating this image he kept a strong connection with a British audience which could identify with him.

Class also plays its part in the appeal of *Zulu*. Despite playing an officer, Lieutenant John Chard, Baker's proletarian credentials are established from the beginning of the film. We first see him stripping off his tunic to get down in a river and help his men to construct a bridge. He is sharply contrasted with Michael Caine's Lieutenant Gonville Bromhead, who we first encounter returning with his servants from a spot of big game hunting. Their initial meeting bristles with class antipathy as the pompous Bromhead entreats Chard to 'carry on with your mud pies'. Cy Endfield shoots the sequence with considerable skill, alternating point-of-view shots between Bromhead mounted on his horse and Chard down in the river, so that we feel the antagonism between them. Although Bromhead has the height advantage, it's apparent who has the moral high ground. These class differences are confirmed by the attitudes of the enlisted men who regard Bromhead as a 'proper gentleman', even if he is English, while Chard is merely an 'officer of engineers'. This theme is mirrored in the depiction of Private Harry Hook, played with relish by James Booth, a working-class malingerer who becomes one of the heroes of Rorke's Drift, even trying to rescue the sergeant who had sent him to the stockade for pilfering.

The most striking aspect of the film is its attempt to marry a stirring tale of military heroism with a liberal critique of colonialism and war. It unquestionably succeeds in the first respect. The film is stunningly shot by Stephen Dade in Technicolor and Super Technirama 70, giving full effect to the scenery of South Africa and the red of the soldier's uniforms. John Barry's music is suitably dramatic and we have a sonorous narration spoken by Richard Burton (Sheldon Hall's book on *Zulu* includes a fascinating account by Cy Endfield of the recording of this in a Paris studio with a well-lubricated Burton). The battle scenes are handled by Endfield with meticulous precision, so that tension is maintained throughout and there is never the descent into confusion which is often a feature of this kind of genre cinema. The film does frequently resemble a western, with its arid landscapes, besieged stockade and cattle stampede. At the same time, we are given a number of reminders of the absurdity and brutality of the whole undertaking. The climactic slaughter of the Zulus is horrifying, as the camera tracks over a mountain of writhing bodies cut down by the British soldiers. The company surgeon, played by Patrick Magee, shouts at Chard: 'Damn all you butchers.' Most telling is the conversation between Chard and Bromhead at the close of the film. When asked how he feels, Bromhead says that he feels sick but also something else: 'I feel ashamed.' Chard reveals that this has been his first taste of action: 'Do you think I could stand this butcher's yard more than once – I told you, I came here to build a bridge.' This could be seen as tokenistic but the effect is powerful, bringing into question precisely why the British troops are there. Undue flag waving is avoided throughout the film and care is taken to emphasise the equal skill of the Zulus as tacticians, as well as their obvious bravery.

Not all the contemporary reviewers responded positively to this complexity in the film, some of them seeing it as a double standard. This was particularly the case with the liberal broadsheets who somewhat hypocrit-ically would have preferred it if the film had been a straightforwardly, gung-ho imperialist saga. John Coleman in the *New Statesman* fumed 'none of this pandering to opposed prejudices – the BOP and the CND – generates much in the way of likelihood'. Penelope Gilliatt in *The Observer* said it was 'like trying to graft a left-wing leaflet on to the Duke of Wellington'. In retrospect, it is precisely this element of contradiction which gives the film its impact and has maintained interest over the years in what might otherwise have seemed a relic from another era. Part of the film's fascination lies in the way it takes the genre of the imperial adventure film, which has a history back into the silent period, and makes it relevant for a 1960s audience less likely to take the British Empire at face value. At least David Robinson in the *Financial Times* acknowledged this, saying 'the way the genre has been modified, however, significantly reflects changing attitudes in the post-war cinema'. More recently, Sheldon Hall's essay 'Monkey Feathers: Defending *Zulu*' makes an eloquent case for the film's richness and depth.

The popular tabloid press had no such qualms, greeting its release with obvious enthusiasm; Clive Barnes in the *Daily Express* described *Zulu* as 'an epic worthy of eleven medals'. The one thing that was beyond argument was the film's phenomenal box office success in the UK. It broke the house record in its initial West End run at The Plaza and on national release set a record for the ABC chain. It was the third-highest grossing film of the year at the British box office, beaten only by the third Bond film, *Goldfinger*, and the film debut of The Beatles in *A Hard Day's Night*. Although it never achieved the same level of success in America, its popularity in Britain was recognised by the American trade paper *Motion Picture Herald* who named Baker as the third most popular star in the UK behind Sean Connery and Cliff Richard. Its popularity in Britain has never really dimmed and it was successfully reissued in cinemas in the early 1970s. It has subsequently become a Bank Holiday favourite for British television broadcasters, guar-anteed to bring in decent audience ratings. Ellen Baker fondly remembers going with Stanley to see the nightly queues waiting outside The Plaza. Whatever else Baker might achieve, he had found a place in the popular consciousness with his first film as a producer.

Speaking to Vincent Kane for BBC Wales in 1975 he reflected on his sixty-odd films and said: 'None of them has affected me in the way this particular film has affected me. Not in terms of the critical and financial success, but because I was so personally involved from the time I made it, after it was shown and I am still involved with it.' That personal engage-ment was reflected in the political and class undercurrents of *Zulu*, but most of all in its celebration of Welsh heroism; its Welsh premier at the Olympia cinema, Cardiff, in March 1964 included a rendition of 'Men of Harlech' by the Ferndale choir conducted again by Ivor Emmanuel. He would no doubt have been delighted at the fact that it still arouses such deep affection more than forty years after he made it.

CHAPTER FIVE

Acting for Losey

Along with Cy Endfield, the other expatriate American film director to have a profound influence on the work of Stanley Baker was Joseph Losey. Baker had first worked with Losey on *Blind Date* (1959) and they went on to make three further films together: *The Criminal* (1960), *Eve* (1962) and finally *Accident* (1967), which for many commentators is the artistic high-water mark in Baker's career. If Endfield's collaboration with Baker produced two of his most lastingly popular films, *Hell Drivers* and *Zulu*, then it was Losey who pushed Baker the actor further than any other director he worked for, drawing from him his strongest performances and breaking the boundaries of the tough-guy persona he had established. According to David Caute, Losey's biographer, the role in *Blind Date* had originally been earmarked for the then largely unknown Peter O'Toole, but a bigger star name was required and the part went to Baker. Losey already knew of Baker and had described him as a young man with 'dark, wavy hair and a great deal of arrogance and machismo'. He proved to be perfect for the part of the dogged, antiestablishment policeman, Inspector Morgan. Ellen Baker remembers Losey and Stanley hitting it off immediately and quickly becoming friends. When Losey began to prepare his next project, *The Criminal*, it was Baker he had in mind for the central role of Johnny Bannion.

Joseph Losey was born on 14 January 1909 in La Crosse, Wisconsin, into a comfortable, middle-class family. After attending private school, he went to Dartmouth College to study medicine but rapidly switched to a liberal arts degree. After completing his course he joined the graduate school at Harvard to study literature. As a student he had already become interested in the theatre and when he left Harvard he moved to New York to pursue this. It was the time of the Great Depression and among the many radical New Deal initiatives introduced by the liberal Roosevelt administration was a series of drama projects intended to give work to unemployed theatre workers and provide greater access to the arts for the general public. Losey, who was increasingly interested in left-leaning political ideas, was attracted by the strong element of social commitment at the core of these projects and became involved with a number of them. He also made several short films funded by the Rockefeller Foundation. After war service, he again took up a career in the professional theatre. In 1947 he achieved acclaim and notoriety when he directed a stage production of Bertolt Brecht's *Galileo* with the British-born actor Charles Laughton in the leading role. He broke into Hollywood by making short films for MGM but moved quickly on to RKO where he made his feature film debut with the anti-war parable *The Boy with Green Hair* (1948). This was followed by a series of smartly handled low budget B-movies, many of them in the crime genre, with which he established a reputation for his taut directing style. Most memorable of these are *The Prowler* (1951) and a remake of Fritz Lang's classic of German expressionist cinema *M* (1951). Unfortunately, the liberal sentiments found in these films, along with his long-standing participation in radical theatre groups and other left-wing political activities, brought him to the attention of Senator Joseph McCarthy's House Un-American Activities Committee and, like Cy Endfield, he was forced to leave his homeland and seek refuge in Britain.

Losey arrived in London in 1952 and soon found that the blacklist was following closely behind him. British producers were reluctant to use blacklisted American filmmakers as this could lead to difficulties when they tried to release films in America. Losey struggled to establish himself and worked initially in television. When he did start to make films again he had to work under various pseudonyms, as did Cy Endfield. His first British films continued the pattern of his American work, with genre subjects predominating. He handled these with the same confidence and individuality he had brought to his films in Hollywood. His British debut was the psychological drama *The Sleeping Tiger* (1954) with Dirk Bogarde. *The Intimate Stranger* (1956), with its story of an American film producer in England, provided him with stronger material and a plot which paralleled his own experiences of persecution. He was not completely at home with the period melodrama *The Gentleman and the Gypsy* (1958), but *Time Without Pity* (1957) and *Blind Date* were thoughtful crime mysteries which demonstrated Losey's cinematic panache, as well as his ability to introduce liberal political undercurrents into low-budget films. It was no surprise that he should find an affinity with a socialist like Baker.

If they shared a similar political outlook, then they were also linked by being outsiders within English cinema of the 1950s. In the 1960s a transformation took place in British filmmaking which was at least partially brought about by the influence of directors, writers and stars who came from abroad. Baker, through his Welshness, and Losey, as an American, both experienced English social life from the outside and had the quality of detached observers. They were also both escaping something: political persecution in Losey's case and poverty in Baker's. As David Caute suggests, Losey invariably used Baker as 'an outsider, the loner who never fully belongs and does not wish to'. Baker became an embodiment of Losey's ambivalent feelings towards the constraints of a British culture he found to be still dominated by class differences, something which had come as a shock to him on his arrival in Britain. For Baker, working with Losey was a revelation. He told Clive James:

> I think that it was Losey who really made me first properly aware about being an actor, how involved an actor should be in what he is doing. Up until that stage everything was full of excitement and full of marvellous things, but acting was just acting . . . he made me aware how responsible an actor should be in relation to a film, how involved an actor should be. I watched him and I thought well, I've never seen a director behave like that before and I watched and watched and I thought well, that's marvellous and if I can have a bit of that, if I can do that and I can get that involved, I think that's good. I think that's right.

After Stanley's death, Ellen wrote to Losey: 'You were the man who made Stanley [. . .] the complete caring professional that he became, and he never forgot this.' The creative results were evident in the striking development of his performances under Losey's direction.

The impetus behind *The Criminal* came from Baker himself. Hammer had sent him a script by one of their leading writers, Jimmy Sangster, based on his own short story. Baker took the screenplay to Losey who liked its basic premise but felt it was too derivative of American prison melodramas and needed reworking. It was then Baker who suggested using the young Liverpudlian playwright Alun Owen to produce a new screenplay (Owen was still four years away from the enormous success of writing the first Beatles film, *A Hard Day's Night*). As with many of Losey's early films, *The Criminal* was made with a tiny budget (just £60,000) and backed by a highly commercial, poverty row producer (in this case Jack Greenwood's Merton Park Studios). Merton Park specialised in cheap but stylish crime films, such as their series of Edgar Wallace mysteries. The film's distributor, Anglo-Amalgamated, had a history of switching between exploitation material and more ambitious art-house projects. They had previously backed Losey's first British film, *The Sleeping Tiger*. Losey seems to have found the mercenary regime of Greenwood difficult to deal with and at one point was sacked by his producer. Baker threatened to leave the film if Losey wasn't reinstated, which he promptly was. However, Anglo-Amalgamated insisted that Losey's original cut of 130 minutes was reduced by thirty-five minutes to get it nearer to their standard feature length of ninety minutes.

Despite the tight budget, the film boasts some surprising credits. It was photographed by the gifted American-born cinematographer Robert Krasker, who had shot *The Third Man* (1949) for director Carol Reed. He managed to give the film a combination of grainy naturalism and heightened stylisation which suited Losey's approach. The film was also the first pairing of Losey with the British composer and jazz musician Johnny Dankworth, who would go on to provide scores for many of his other 1960s films. Dankworth's wife, Cleo Laine, performed the haunting vocals for the film's melancholy theme song. These elements gave the film a sophistication beyond the usual ambitions of Merton Park's output.

Anglo-Amalgamated came into their own in marketing the film. They came up with a strategy to build a reputation for the film as 'the toughest picture ever made in Britain'. The poster campaign certainly backed this up, with brooding images of Baker looking sullen and various shots of him with fists flying. His image is accompanied by the caption 'WANTED – By the girl who loved him! – By the gang who hated him! – By the police who pursued him!' They also emphasised Baker's increasing sex symbol status by including pictures of him bare-chested and by providing his female co-star Margit Saad with the caption 'She loved him and didn't care what she did to prove it.' The love story was actually only included at the insistence of the producers and over Losey's objections. Baker's new star status is also reiterated by his name being over the title in type of almost equivalent size. It is clear that Losey felt constricted by the attitude of Merton Park towards the whole venture. He said: 'We got a script which had a great deal of point and was very real in its people and its speech, but which didn't hold together as well as it should structurally because we were forced to retain a melodramatic structure none of us was really interested in.'

The film's narrative certainly strains credibility, despite its strongly realistic approach to depicting life inside prison. Baker's Johnny Bannion leaves jail only to commit another robbery which lands him back behind bars again. He is then involved in a game of cat-and-mouse until he finally escapes, setting off to retrieve the buried loot from the robbery and rescue his girl from the other gang member (Sam Wanamaker) who has kidnapped her as a way of forcing Bannion to hand over the money to him. Losey's real interest lies in showing the failings of the prison system to offer any alternative to an individual like Bannion, who is shown to be an intelligent man, with a moral side; his Catholicism is referred to several times. Losey said: 'This is what I tried to present in Bannion, that this is a waste, that the prison system hasn't changed, that it doesn't help.' Bannion is caught between two equally destructive forces. Behind bars, there is the corruption of the prison system itself, as personified by the ineffectual governor (Noel

Willman) and a psychotic warder, played with manic glee by Patrick Magee, whose principle pleasure appears to be encouraging the inmates to beat each other up. The scene of inmates walking circles in the prison yard is positively Dickensian. Once on the outside, Bannion discovers that organised crime operates with the ethics of capitalist big business. Wanamaker's character, who effectively represents the unseen face of a corporate gangster who they are all ultimately working for, tells Bannion: 'With us it's a team, it's business, but your sort doesn't fit into an organisation.' The film is, however, undermined by the schematic way in which this message is put across. Later in his career Losey would attract equal praise and criticism for his baroque directing style and elements of that surface here. The claustrophobia of prison is brilliantly suggested with fluid camerawork, including gliding crane shots, and abrupt cuts from wide shot to extreme close-up, but the use of deep focus, acute angles, montage editing and expressionistic lighting, sometimes all in the same sequence, is sometimes overpowering, inducing a tone of escalating hysteria into the film.

The press response was mainly hostile, with Losey taking most of the blame. Many of the reviews were simply dismissive, but others focused on the stylistic excesses and melodramatic overstatement of the narrative. Richard Roud for *Sight and Sound* was a rare champion of the film, describing Losey as having a 'control over his material, his actors, and his visuals more rigorous and more strikingly personal than before. In *The Criminal* he has at last found his way to the top.' The film obtained a good deal of critical attention in France where Losey was rapidly gaining cult status among serious critics on journals like *Cahier du Cinema*. Baker escaped much of the criticism, largely obtaining approving notices and also achieving greater exposure in France than he had done previously. The film was screened at the Edinburgh Festival where it won a Diploma of Merit, but it didn't make much impact at the British box office or in America where it suffered as a result of poor distribution, being released with the unfortunate title of *The Concrete Jungle*. Subsequent reassessments of the film have found much to admire, particularly in Baker's performance. David Berry sees it as another variation of his isolated loner, with Baker 'still riveting, suggesting the man's psychosis, barely suppressed rage, and latent power'. Berry attributes the film's initial failure to the unconvincing development of the romantic subplot, suggesting that the more fascinating relationship is actually that between Bannion and his alter ego, Patrick Magee's demented warder.

Baker's performance is startlingly extreme. As David Berry notes, he is given little with which to make the character sympathetic. Instead we are attracted by his energy and ferocity. This is seen particularly when he and

Magee trade insults and taunt each other towards violence. He takes on a messianic quality when he arrives back in prison to shouts of 'Home, sweet home' from the other inmates; he bursts into near hysterical laughter. His toughness is such that he can dispense with the two thugs who set on him in his cell without any difficulties. The tone of unbridled aggression is enhanced by a haircut which gives him an unpleasantly bullish appearance. The film also makes an implicit link between his violence and a kind of sexual charisma. For the first time, Baker portrays a sexually attractive figure. His bachelor pad is decorated with images of half-naked women and he seems to draw in Margit Saad's Suzanne with magnetic prowess; retiring to his bedroom he discovers her waiting naked in his bed. Poor Jill Bennett is driven half insane by the prospect of losing him. Baker was quick to acknowledge how he benefited from working with Losey on the film: 'When shooting begins, it's not simply a matter of getting up and going to the studio. For instance, Losey might, after the studio, talk to you for two or three hours about the film, that or the next day's shooting. As an actor, you can't refuse this sort of man who gives himself completely to his films.'

One fascinating element of the production was the opportunity it gave Baker to fraternise with genuine criminals. He met and became friends with Albert Dime, who Losey described as 'a huge, staggeringly handsome man who drove around in a smashing white convertible with black upholstery'. He also happened to be a real-life version of Johnny Bannion and Baker ended up basing his performance on him. Stanley took to hanging around with him and frequenting the same East End pubs, where other gangsters like Frankie Fraser could be found, along with the boxer Henry Cooper. He seems to have felt some affinity with these outlaws who might be seen, for those inclined to be sympathetic, as working-class heroes, of a sort. He retained an interest in, and an instinctive empathy for, outsiders of all descriptions. In a somewhat tongue-in-cheek television interview, Frankie Fraser suggested that Baker would have made a fine bank robber: 'That could have been him, tough, he wouldn't have cared. It's a shame he became an actor, foolish. He should have come down our road.' There was also the thrill of danger for a man who enjoyed to gamble. Ellen recalls how he got his comeuppance for this when some of Dime's cronies arranged a stunt to see what reaction they could get from Baker. In the smoky backroom of a pub, as they all played poker, a staged fight broke out and knives were pulled. According to Henry Cooper, Stanley first hid under the table and then couldn't be seen for dust as he headed out the door. During the making of the film he did, however, get to show his mettle. His co-star Sam Wanamaker was a struggling, virtually unknown actor. His polite enquiries as to whether he might be allowed to keep the suits he wore in the film were met with a flat refusal from the producers. Baker's response on hearing this was to head on to the set after completion of the shoot and raid the wardrobe department on Wanamaker's behalf.

Baker and Losey's third venture together, *Eve*, was to prove a traumatic, fraught affair both on and off the screen. Between *The Criminal* and *Eve*, Baker had made his commercial breakthrough to international recognition with *The Guns of Navarone*. At the same time, Losey had completed *The Damned* (1961) for Hammer, an idiosyncratic Cold War parable about a group of children contaminated by radiation. *Eve* was developed as a project by the producers Robert and Raymond Hakim and was adapted from a novel by the American writer James Hadley Chase. Using their Rome-based production company Interopa to fund the film (in collaboration with Paris Film in France), they already had both Stanley Baker and French star Jeanne Moreau on board when they approached the French New Wave director Jean-Luc Godard to direct. Godard was apparently happy enough with Baker but wouldn't countenance working with Moreau, and so it was at Stanley Baker's suggestion that Losey be brought in as a replacement. The story's original American settings were transferred to Rome and Venice, and the film was to be shot by an Italian crew with the addition of Losey's preferred editor Reginald Mills, and designer Richard Macdonald, both brought in from Britain. Losey had Chase's original pulp novel reworked first by the Hollywood screenwriter Hugo Butler and then by the playwright Evan Jones, who he had collaborated with on *The Damned*. Losey seems to have regarded the film as his chance to escape the limitations of the British B-movie and claim his place among the major figures of European art cinema such as Antonioni and Fellini. He even secured as his cinematographer Gianni di Venanzo, who had worked with both of those Italian maestros.

Losey enjoyed the process of filming in Italy and consequently dragged out the shooting to an inordinate length, continually straying from the script to include each new picturesque location he had discovered. He also clashed repeatedly with the Hakim brothers over the direction the film was taking. Notoriously, at one point during the cutting of the film Losey discovered that the Hakims had brought in their own editor over a weekend break to recut the film without him. His reaction was to pin Robert Hakim to a wall. Losey's own original cut of the film ran to an indulgent 155 minutes and he initially agreed to the Hakims' request that he reduce its running time; they had already withdrawn the film from entry in the Venice Film Festival. The version that eventually premiered in Paris in the autumn of 1962, to a highly negative response, had been reduced to roughly 116 minutes. Losey blamed the poor reception on the re-editing of the film and wrote to the Hakims requesting that they restore it to something nearer its original length. Far from agreeing to his demands, they cut the film still further to around 103 minutes for its 1963 British release. The version that eventually arrived in America as *Eva* in 1965 seems to have been about that length. Losey used the press to protest against the Hakims' handling of his film. A report in *Variety* in November of 1962 stated: 'Joseph Losey would like it to be known as a matter of record that his latest, "Eve", which stars Jeanne Moreau and Stanley Baker, is circulating with 25 minutes of film removed which he wants restored.' Losey persuaded Baker, Moreau, and the film's composer, Michel Legrand, to join his protests. The *Daily Mail* reported their request to have their names removed from all publicity and even from the film's titles as 'unprecedented in film history'. Baker was quoted as saying: 'The film, as it is being shown now in England, has been emasculated. For some reason Mr Hakim has seen fit to chop 50 minutes out of it.' Raymond Hakim was reported as saying: '*Eve* was originally supposed to be an action film, running for 1½ hours. But Mr. Losey let it run much longer and made it into something else.'

Ellen remembers the process of making *Eve* as a difficult experience: 'The filming just went on and on. Joe was completely obsessive about it and kept returning to things again and again. I thought it would never end. Stanley and Joe were great friends but Stanley hated making that film.' She recalled that it was Baker who restrained Losey from inflicting any greater violence on Robert Hakim in their cutting-room altercation. Such was the protracted nature of shooting *Eve* that their fourth child was conceived and born before it was eventually released in Britain. In honour of the fact, they named their new son Adam. With the baby due at any moment, Losey reluctantly allowed Baker to visit home for a few days. With no sign of the baby arriving, he was required to head for the airport and go back to Italy. Stopping on the way at a favourite pub for a farewell drink with friends, he took a phone call which rapidly summoned him back home for Adam's belated appearance. Despite Losey, he had managed to be at home for his son's birth after all. When Stanley and Ellen eventually saw the film at its London premiere they were both disappointed, quietly leaving the cinema when the film was barely half over. To this day she has not seen the restored version. It was largely as an act of loyalty to his friend that Baker had joined in the protests against the butchering of the film. To add to the strain of the filming, Jeanne Moreau lived up to her billing as a capricious free spirit, making life on set difficult. She was pursuing an affair which took her away to Paris at every opportunity. When she and Baker were given the Valentino Award in 1974, Ellen went to the ceremony with their son Glyn (Stanley couldn't make it) and during proceedings Moreau took Glyn to one side to ask him to take a belated apology for her behaviour back to her old co-star.

The film met with a decidedly mixed response from British reviewers on its release. The tabloids generally dismissed it as pretentious, as did some of the broadsheets, but the film also had its supporters. Isabel Quigly in *The Spectator* conceded that *Eve* was 'three-fifths preposterous', yet she was also impressed by Losey's directorial flair:

> He is one of those rare directors who seem not to have come to the cinema from outside, but to have been born inside it, somehow to float in the medium, to live cinematically; incapable of making a dull frame or a meaningless image and often, in fact, jamming the screen so tight with meaning, reference, nudges and suggestions that you are almost irritated at having only two eyes, one brain and a second or two to absorb it.

A number of other commentators praised the film's ambition and style, even if they felt that it was overindulgent. As the unnamed reviewer in *The Times* put it, 'Mr Losey is almost incapable of making an uninteresting film. Bad, yes, but uninteresting never.' Several critics acknowledged that the film had been cut, although the review in *The Times* suggested that it needed more cutting. Moreau was almost universally admired, with most reviews regarding the film as having been made largely to showcase her bewitching star qualities. This was undeniably the approach taken by the film's British distributor, Gala, whose promotional campaign almost entirely centred on Moreau, featuring such lurid taglines as 'A temptress – Eve led men to complete degradation. Eve destroyed all men who crossed her path.' If the critics were in awe of Moreau, they were confused by the casting of Baker. At this stage in his career, he was still largely regarded as an action hero and tough guy, not as a serious actor. Some felt that the role was beyond him, but others were impressed. Alexander Walker in the *Evening Standard* found his performance to be a revelation, describing him as having 'the fierce compression of a blowlamp'.

In April 1966, as part of a tribute season for cinematographer Gianni di Venanzo who had recently died, the National Film Theatre tracked down a Scandinavian copy of *Eve* which was about fifteen minutes longer than the British release version and probably similar to the print initially screened in France to such poor reviews. Although the programme notes issued with the screening contain numerous factual inaccuracies, Losey is quoted as saying: 'This print contains nothing that I don't want in it, misses certain things that I do, but it is enough for you to make a judgement in terms of performances, mine as well as the actors, script, style and intention, and this has never been so before.' The reviews for this screening are noticeably better than for the film's original British release but still far from ecstatic. Many critics found the film too personal, and Baker was still picked out as being miscast. Kenneth Tynan in *The Observer* suggested the part needed a more sensitive actor like Montgomery Clift. He also criticised a number of Losey's directorial flourishes, but nonetheless concluded by saying that *Eve* 'ranks close to *The Servant* on the high plateau of Losey's best work, and I wish it a wider showing'. Baker himself was relatively equivocal on the subject when he later told Clive James: 'I've seen both versions – I believe Losey's version is far better than the producer's. But I mean that's personal taste.'

That version of the film was preserved by the British Film Institute and is currently available on the Kino International DVD release of the film in the United States. The DVD actually provides viewers with both the American theatrical release version at 103 minutes and the BFI's Swedish/Finnish print at 119 minutes. This version has Swedish and Finnish subtitles on screen and is a poor quality print, but it does allow a comparison to be made between these two versions, although we shall presumably never know what Losey's 155 minute cut was like. The extra sixteen minutes mainly consist of bridging sequences between major scenes, and there are altera-tions to the soundtrack. The American release version is often choppy in its editing and the transitions in the soundtrack between different pieces of music are frequently jarring. In the longer version this is smoothed out, with the musical transitions occurring rhythmically. The inclusion of the addi-tional bridging sequences makes the film flow better, as well as creating a sustained mood, but it also adds length to a film which already feels drawn out at 103 minutes. Sadly, it is not the discovery of a lost cinematic masterpiece. The film remains substantially flawed, but fascinating in either version.

The roles of Eve and Tyvian Jones were deliberately tailored to suit Moreau and Baker. Tyvian Jones is a writer from south Wales and a former miner who has now achieved literary fame with a successful novel which has been made into a film. At one point he confesses to having only spent a short time down the pit while his brother was the real miner, which is obviously not that far from the truth. Baker signals the extent of his personal affinity with the character by exaggerating his Welsh accent in some scenes and by singing several songs in Welsh. There are references to the lingering influence of his Welsh upbringing and in particular the power of the Chapel. Moreau's iconic status is heavily emphasised, especially in an extraordinary four-minute take when the camera follows her as she wanders round Baker's apartment, removing her stockings, putting on a Billie Holliday record, drying her hair from the rain, examining the room and looking in the mirror, before finally plunging into a bath. It's easy to read the film as a contemplation of Moreau's charismatic beauty but the story is not really about her; it is about what she means to Baker's character and consequently we see her almost entirely through his eyes. Tyvian Jones is revealed to be a fake, whose success has come through stealing his dead brother's manuscript. For whatever psychological reasons, perhaps guilt or insecurity, he is driven to destroy himself, which he achieves through his relentless pursuit of the mercenary, uncaring Eve. He wrecks his marriage and inadvertently causes the death of his wife, but still crawls back for more abuse. His degradation is complete after Eve whips him and throws him out of her apartment into the gutter, only for him to reappear again, begging to be allowed to see her one more time. She refuses and sends him packing with the film's memorable last line: 'Bloody Welshman'.

Baker conveys the character with considerable emotional power, despite the essentially melodramatic nature of what takes place. It is a richly complex, layered performance which unpicks the stereotype of the macho Welshman. His new found sex symbol status is, nonetheless, underlined by the scenes of him waterskiing early in the film, but what is most striking are his sudden changes of mood. He switches startlingly from moments of quiet tenderness to bitter cynicism, to explosions of rage, in an alarmingly convincing manner. This is portrayed only occasionally by actual aggression but more often through his cat-like movements and the pitch of his voice. One of Baker's strengths as an actor was his ability to suggest inner tension, a thinly concealed ferocity, which is used to impressive effect here. He is aided in this by Losey's baroque visual style, all gliding tracking shots and quirky angles. The nightclub scene with its black male dancer in a white mask, and the sequence of Moreau shutting her door in Baker's face with the camera peering down from a perilously high angle are memorable. Losey skilfully conjures a world of affluent decadence, depicting an artistic international jet set gathered in glamorous Venice and Rome, but mired in inertia and moral decay. Where the film capsizes is in the too personal meaning it seems to have held for Losey. David Caute quotes Losey as saying: 'It was almost an orgasm, and it was probably . . . self-indulgent . . . it was like a coitus interruptus . . . a moment when I broke out, exposed myself and was completely vulnerable.' Losey apparently projected his feelings about himself onto the character of Tyvian Jones, both in the hopeless, unreciprocated fascination with Moreau and in the consequent self-loathing. Caute suggests that Baker was effectively Losey's 'fall guy', saddled with the job of standing in for the director. The unconvincing narrative and characterisations, especially of Eve herself, simply can't accommodate Losey's attempt to load the film with significance, a fact not helped by the heavy-handedness of some of his stylistic excesses.

After such a bruising experience it was perhaps understandable that Baker didn't work again with Losey until 1966 with the making of *Accident* (he was, in any case, pouring much of his creative energy into the production of *Zulu*). Fortunately it turned out to be a creative highpoint for both of them. In 1963 Losey had made his breakthrough to international critical acclaim with *The Servant*. Adapted from Robin Maugham's novel by the playwright Harold Pinter, the film had allowed Losey to fully explore his fascination with the British class system. His direction, with the exception of the final orgy scene, was tightly disciplined and he drew fine performances from James Fox and Dirk Bogarde as the master and servant who play out their destructive power games. After the sober anti-war film *King and Country* (1964) and the camp James Bond pastiche *Modesty Blaise* (1966), both featuring Bogarde, Losey was teamed with Pinter again for *Accident*. The film is an adaptation of Nicholas Mosley's novel about life among the dons of an Oxford college and was initially backed by the American producer Sam Spiegel. However, fearing that Spiegel might intervene too much in the making of the film, Losey and Pinter bought the adaptation rights from him and eventually found financial backing from a combination of the National Film Finance Corporation and Sidney Box's London Independent Productions. The film was shot partly on location, including sequences filmed at Magdalen and St John's colleges at Oxford, as well as in studio interior sets meticulously created by Losey's designer Carmen Dillon. Despite poor weather, skilful editing and Gerry Fisher's Eastmancolor cinematography managed to suggest the languorous warmth of a long summer.

One of the strengths of the film is the interplay between Baker and Bogarde, as two contrasting dons who compete in their academic careers and in their desires for a female student, Anna, played by Jacqueline Sassard. Bogarde's Stephen is a seemingly hesitant, accident prone, ineffectual man, who is later revealed to possess a darker, callous side. By contrast, Baker's Charley is self-confident, even arrogant, a successful and ambitious academic who appears regularly on television. He seduces Anna, inducing anger and envy in equal measure from Stephen. As Peter Stead suggests, the story 'is essentially an exercise in which two dons tear themselves apart, and to sustain this Losey merely exploited the off-screen tension between his two leading actors, the cerebral, refined, elegant, urbane and very English Dirk Bogarde and the physical, athletic, opportunistic Baker'. Bogarde was initially unhappy with the casting of Baker: 'I was against Stanley – too thuggish, too much the working-class lad. He arrived in a toupee and a lot of make-up and was always doing his eyelashes for the first two days. After that he was terrific, wonderful – I was very fond of him.' While on the set he described their working relationship in rather ostentatious terms as 'a marvellous matching of contrasted flavours, a real strong country Cheddar and a more delicate, insidious Demi-sel'. Quite how Baker might have felt at being likened to a cheese is best left to the imagination. When Clive James later asked how he had achieved such a 'marvellous brittle antagonism with Bogarde' he replied in typically diplomatic form: 'Well, that's just acting. That is the business of acting. It's lovely, you know, acting, when you get that involved because the lines are so good, because the situation is so good; it's wonderful for an actor to go into a situation like that. If you can't do it then you're not an actor.'

Ellen remembers Stanley and Dirk Bogarde actually getting on well during the shoot, despite the fact that they had not been on the best terms on their previous film together, *Campbell's Kingdom*. There was a growing respect between the two actors, despite their temperamental differences. She recalled:

> Dirk always said he found the experience one of the most challenging of his whole career, really tough. But Stanley was fine. He found the role straightforward enough to play and Harold Pinter was on set a lot of the time. He gave Stanley advice which really helped him to understand the character and bring him alive.

Baker also enjoyed working with the young Michael York. Ellen explained: 'Stanley always liked to encourage actors who were new to films. He had done that with Michael Caine on *Zulu* and he got on very well with Michael York too.' Whatever their personal view of each other, it seems that for Losey, Bogarde and Baker provided two contrasting personas which could usefully be set against each other, with Baker's instinctive directness working dramatically against the more studied, brittle appearance of Bogarde. As David Caute puts it, 'Stanley Baker was an elemental actor relying on brooding menace, physically assertive, a cocksure style with women, always himself.'

If *The Servant* was a dissection of the power struggle between the classes, then *Accident* restricts its focus to the moral degeneration of the British middle class. Outwardly, both Stephen and Charley are respectable, civilised men. Both university lecturers, both married with children, they are witty, literate and intellectually sophisticated. But as the surface of their lives is scraped away, an entirely different inner life is revealed. Charley is selfish and a bully. He abandons his family to undertake an affair with Anna, a wealthy foreign student years younger than himself. He then treats her with a similar disdain, ordering her around like a chattel. Stephen is mired in jealousy at Charley's success, with women and as a media-friendly academic. He wants Anna every bit as much as Charley but doesn't have his friend's ruthless self-confidence, leaving him watching from the sidelines, encouraging their affair. He seems to take a vicarious pleasure in what Charley does, allowing the lovers to use his house to meet while his own wife is in hospital having their baby and he is away for the weekend. The sham of both their lives is revealed in the final third of the film, as Anna deserts the increasingly pathetic, deluded Charley and Stephen's inner violence is exposed when he appears to molest a traumatised Anna following the car accident which has killed her fellow student and fiancé, William (Michael York). Losey heightens the feeling that we are looking in, almost voyeuristically, at a corrupt social milieu by using various distancing effects. The camera is deliberately kept back from the action in long shot, much of the dialogue is coldly banal, Johnny Dankworth's score is used sparingly, and there are lengthy takes where characters carry out mundane tasks. In one sequence, where Stephen meets an old flame (Delphine Seyrig) in London, the sound is non-synchronous, creating a dream-like feeling of dislocation. By Losey's standards, the direction is almost chillingly restrained, in keeping with his subject.

The film's central sequence, the long, lazy Sunday spent by the central characters at Stephen's house, typifies the overall tone. Charley arrives in his flashy sports car and immediately makes his presence felt by playing football with Stephen's young son. The summer sun is sweltering as they lounge on the lawn and then play a game of tennis. Stephen goes for a walk with Anna in the country which is charged with sexual longing. Charley flirts with Stephen's heavily pregnant wife, Rosalind (Vivien Merchant). As the beer and whisky flow, and the afternoon turns to evening, William gets drunk, while Stephen and Charley become embroiled in a bitter exchange of polite insults. When a bleary Stephen finally goes to bed he accidentally refers to his sleeping wife as Anna and then breaks down in tears of guilt. Little is said directly and yet we are aware that these people are falling apart in front of our eyes. In the midst of this, Baker takes on the role of devil's advocate, stating bluntly what the others are only thinking. Having asked William to describe what he sees around him in the garden (he replies in straightforward terms), Charley explains what *he* sees: 'You could go so much further. Rosalind is pregnant. Stephen is having an affair with a girl at Oxford. He has reached that age where he can't keep his hands off girls at Oxford. He feels guilty, of course, so he makes up a story. This story.' The immediate rise in tension is palpable. In a film which could easily have drifted into ambiguous inertia, it is Charley who gives the film its edge. Baker brings to proceedings a fierce honesty, a disruptive hint of danger. It is the most complex, subtle and controlled acting performance of his film career.

The critical response to the film, and Baker's contribution, was almost uniformly positive. Some commentators, such as the reviewer in the *Sunday Express*, still refused to accept that Baker could be cast in such intellectually challenging material but this attitude increasingly looked like simple snobbery. Nina Hibbin in the *Morning Star* said that 'both actors give performances of faultless integrity', while Ann Pacey in *The Sun* singled out Baker saying: 'I do not think I have ever seen Stanley Baker do anything better.' They were the best notices Baker had yet received. Praising *Accident* as 'the most intellectually exciting and absorbing film I have watched in months and the finest work to date of director Joseph Losey', Alexander Walker, writing in the London *Evening Standard*, went on to say:

> The revelation of the film is Stanley Baker. Almost unrecognisable for the first few seconds behind library spectacles and in an anti-Baker posture of sprawling donnishness among the university periodicals, he swiftly, subtly develops the prickly ambiguities of a man who can't help hurting others. Watch the myriad little mean flicks of animosity he manifests in jokey but jealous ways. I predict that *Accident* will do for Stanley Baker what *The Servant* did for Bogarde.

Accident was nominated in four categories at the BAFTAs and for a Golden Globe. The Writers' Guild of Great Britain gave their Merit Scroll to Harold Pinter and although the film missed out on the coveted Palme d'Or at Cannes, it picked up the Jury Prize as compensation. The accolades were a recognition of the distance that Baker had come with Losey and of his newly acquired status as a serious and gifted actor.

Baker was, regrettably, never to work with Losey again. They remained friends and, as Losey's letters indicate, kept in touch, but a distance opened up between them. Baker was to become increasingly occupied with his new career as a producer, while Losey pursued various, increasingly personal film projects in continental Europe. Losey's correspondence shows that he occasionally wrote to Baker, on one occasion asking if he could give a friend a job on one of his productions, while Stanley's son, Martin, reciprocated by approaching Losey for work. None of these requests appear to have been successful. Losey wrote to Baker to bemoan the fact that they hadn't seen each other in years, ticking him off for not returning his calls or replying to his letters. A letter he sent to Baker on 1 June 1972 is especially striking and is reproduced here in full:

Dear Stanley,

Years go by without seeing you and without any word. I am aware of your various activities, but among them nothing of you as an actor or a person.

The other night, rather against my will, I found myself watching ACCIDENT from beginning to end. I think your performance is absolutely superb – in fact, it stands up better than any in the picture.

What a pity you are not digging deeper into your extraordinary talents and what a pity that we never speak or meet.

Love

J. Losey

Instead of following the creative path as an actor that he had opened up with Losey, Baker turned instead to the behind the scenes role of executive and film entrepreneur. Losey obviously regretted this and we can only speculate on what might have been if Baker had chosen a different direction.

CHAPTER SIX

From Actor to Producer

When Stanley Baker first turned to producing his intentions were straight-forward enough; *Zulu* was to be the most personal project of his career to date and he was not going to leave it in the hands of anyone else. Diamond Films, the company he established with Cy Endfield and Bob Porter, was a means to a specific end and had little life beyond the filming of *Zulu*. However, producing the film whetted his appetite for this new role and set his career off in a direction which was to dominate his working life for the next ten years. It is clear that working with Joseph Losey had enabled him to see how filmmaking looked from behind the camera, as well as opening his eyes to its full artistic potential. Watching his television interview with Vincent Kane, there is a real passion and commitment as he tells him:

> If I appear in a film that has any value at all and my part in it, my characterisation, my work in it, has any value, then on one night, throughout the world, millions of people will see it. It means an immense amount to me because I believe that filmmaking is that sort of a medium. Used properly, filmmaking can have a wonderful influence on the way we lead our lives.

But Baker was a pragmatist, as well as an idealist. He told *Photoplay* magazine: 'I became a producer because whenever I read stories or scripts that seemed worthwhile material for films, I used to pass them on to other people. I began to wonder: why not me? Why shouldn't I make these films myself?' The process of making *Zulu* had proven to be exhilarating. He had become engrossed in the planning and with the attention to detail required to bring it to the screen. He had also proved to himself that he could actually do it, and be successful. The popularity of *Zulu* at the box office was sufficient vindication of his self-belief.

Someone else who was impressed by his abilities as a producer and star was Joseph E. Levine, the American backer of *Zulu*. Levine was keen to work with Baker again, especially on further African-set adventures which might promise the same kind of financial returns as *Zulu*. The first consequence of this for Baker was the starring role in *Dingaka* (1965). The film was made by Levine's own production company, Embassy, and released through the distribution deal he had struck up with Paramount. It was again shot on location in South Africa with a cast and crew which were largely sourced locally. The film was the second to be made by the independent South African filmmaker James Uys who produced, wrote and directed it. He later became the first South African filmmaker to achieve major international success with the comedy *The Gods Must be Crazy* (1981). *Dingaka* tells of a tribesman, played powerfully by Ken Gampu, who he believes responsible for killing his daughter. Baker is cast as the sympathetic barrister who defends him and tries to explain to a white jury the codes and traditions of a culture which they do not wish to understand. The film doesn't entirely avoid National Geographic-style exoticism and was garishly marketed by Embassy to play on the visual attractions of the location shooting in Cinemascope and Technicolor. The courtroom proceedings are also inevitably melodramatic, but the film is sincere in its liberal intentions and was a brave undertaking by all concerned. However, its very limited success did not go anywhere near replicating the impact of *Zulu*.

Levine belonged to an established tradition of maverick American producers who operated on the fringes of the Hollywood studio system and were often characterised by their flamboyant showmanship. He had dragged himself up from an impoverished childhood, working in a variety of jobs before entering the industry as the manager of a cinema in New Haven, Connecticut. Moving on from distribution into production, he showed an uncanny ability to gauge what audiences wanted which rapidly made him rich. Perhaps his liking for Baker grew out of a recognition that they shared similar personal histories, both having had to fight their way out of poverty to success. Bob Porter, Stanley's long-time friend and collaborator, remembers Levine with affection:

> He was a rough, New York diamond, but a wonderful man. He worked on instinct. When he believed in the people he was dealing with, he would really back them up. If you could show him that you had a project or a script that you really had faith in and were excited by, then he would trust you. He had enormous belief in me and in Stanley.

Levine's faith in Baker was quickly translated into something concrete when he subsequently agreed a deal for him to produce and star in three further films which would be backed by Embassy.

The first of these was another African adventure, *Sands of the Kalahari* (1965). The film was to mark the final collaboration between Baker and Cy Endfield. As with *Zulu*, they produced the film together through Pendennis, the independent company which Endfield had established in the late 1950s. Bob Porter acted as associate producer for Pendennis and Joe Levine was executive producer handling the distribution end of the deal with Paramount. Endfield wrote the screenplay himself, adapting the novel by

William Mulvihill. Unfortunately, the production was beset with problems before the cameras even turned. Baker had succeeded in interesting his old friend Richard Burton in appearing in the film. They had discussed working together on a number of occasions over the years; the press even reported their plans to film a Dylan Thomas short story in the early 1960s. Burton was to be accompanied by his wife, Elizabeth Taylor, as his co-star. Not surprisingly, this generated a good deal of press excitement, but the world's most glamorous couple, for whatever reasons, never did appear in the film. Instead, the young British actress Susannah York was signed for the leading female role, while Hollywood star George Peppard was cast in Burton's place. The problems didn't end there, as Ellen Baker recalled: 'I flew out to join Stanley on location and as I got there George Peppard was literally on his way back home on the next plane out. As I arrived, he left.' Bizarrely, Peppard seems to have been alarmed by the baboons who were to be among his co-stars in the film, as well as being irritated by the fact that he was not allowed to use his own gun in the film's action scenes. He also took a dislike to Cy Endfield. Baker didn't hold anything back in informing the press about his annoyance with Peppard: 'In all my career I have never seen a more destructive act. The whole unit could have been put out of work. If I ever run across him again I will spit in his face.' Alan Bates was approached but was unavailable. Belatedly, another American actor, Stuart Whitman, was brought in as a last minute replacement. Further difficulties then arose during the shoot; as Baker recounted to *Photoplay*; there were problems with the unruly baboons, legions of deadly snakes and scorpions to contend with, and the sand at the location turned out to be an unacceptable shade of grey. Tonnes of sand in the required hue were brought in by truck, only then to be washed away by a freak thunderstorm. Nonetheless, the magazine reported, Baker had managed to bring the film in on time and within budget.

Despite these difficulties, the finished film is an effective meditation on the violent survival instincts of human beings, framed as a thrilling adventure yarn. Baker, Whitman and York are among the passengers stranded when their aircraft ditches in the desert. With them are a number of notable character actors including Nigel Davenport and Harry Andrews. Baker's character, Mike Bain, is deliberately contrasted with Whitman's, Brian O'Brien. Bain appears at first to be a drunken reprobate but is soon revealed to be the voice of reason, a decent man who wants to preserve civilised values whatever the circumstances, while O'Brien is exposed as a ruthless survivalist who has no qualms about eliminating the others in order to save himself. The presence of the baboons adds an extra element of threat. The narrative development is highly melodramatic, but the film is impressively shot in widescreen and colour by Erwin Hillier, making much of the desolate sandscapes and maintaining an unsettling atmosphere throughout. Joseph Losey's favoured composer, Johnny Dankworth, provides a stark score, and the film is handled with Endfield's usual terse efficiency. If there is a weakness it lies in the roles taken by Whitman and Baker, which might more successfully have been reversed. Whitman is never sufficiently menacing as O'Brien and Baker is slightly wasted in the more conventionally heroic role. It is easy to imagine what he might have made of the calculating, single-minded O'Brien. Nevertheless, the film builds to a memorable climax with Baker and York rescued, while Whitman is left to the mercy of the baboons. The ending is ambiguous, leaving the audience to decide whether Whitman, who we see killing the chief baboon, has become their leader or has been eaten alive by them. The underlying message about the brutal inner nature of mankind is conveyed rather heavy-handedly in some portentous dialogue about the collapse of civilisation, as well as through the film's biblical overtones (the plane is brought down by a plague of locusts). The publicity material for the film made sure the audience were in no doubt as to what this was all about, with the posters informing us that 'It's kill or be killed in the *Sands of the Kalahari*.'

In retrospect, *Sands of the Kalahari* is a striking film which at least partly fulfils its ambitions, but contemporary critics and audiences were not so kind. Box office returns were disappointing and the reviews were mainly poor. Some of the tabloids found it exciting enough, and there was praise for the cinematography, but there was also much hilarity at the film's pretensions, as well as for Susannah York's role as token sex interest. Baker the actor was let off lightly but Baker the producer took plenty of criticism, as did Cy Endfield for what was perceived as clumsily overstated direction. Kenneth Tynan in *The Observer* commented that 'the notion of man as a natural killer and power-seeker deserves a more formidable interpreter than Mr Endfield' and suggested that Endfield should steer clear of his typewriter for a while. Tynan inadvertently got his wish. Endfield's widow later told Sheldon Hall that the film's critical and commercial failure seriously damaged his plans for several further projects with Levine and he found it increasingly difficult to get any other ideas off the ground. Endfield's film career never fully recovered and he only completed two further assignments as a director. It was a sad end to his working relationship with Baker and it is probably better to think of their earlier successes, particularly with *Zulu*. Back in 1964 the quality of their work together had been recognised by the Cinémathèque Française who staged a tribute to Baker and Endfield in Paris, timed to coincide with the French release of *Zulu*.

Baker's next undertaking for Levine was a happier affair. Parted from Endfield, *Robbery* (1967) was the first release for Baker's new company,

11. Baker's greatest success, as Lt John Chard in *Zulu* (1964). Courtesy of Paramount Pictures.

12. The handsome leading man. Courtesy of Lady Ellen Baker.

13. Perhaps his finest performance, in Losey's *Accident* (1967). London Independent producers, courtesy of the Kobal Collection.

14. The producer and star, making *Robbery* (1967). Courtesy of Lady Ellen Baker.

15. On one of his regular charity appearances. Courtesy of Lady Ellen Baker.

16. With Ursula Andress in *Perfect Friday* (1970). Sunnymede, courtesy of the Kobal Collection.

17. With Ellen. Courtesy of Lady Ellen Baker.

18. The Sir Stanley Baker Lounge at Ferndale Rugby Club.
Courtesy of Robert Shail.

19. Stanley Baker's ashes were scattered on the
hillside overlooking Ferndale's rugby
ground. Courtesy of Robert Shail.

Oakhurst Productions. With offices at 34 South Molton Street, London W1, Oakhurst was set up by Baker in collaboration with Bob Porter and a new business partner, Michael Deeley. Deeley, who was born in 1932, had started in television as an editor in the mid 1950s and was co-producer of *The Mukkinese Battlehorn* (1955), a short film made by The Goons. In the early 1960s he become general manager of Woodfall Films, the company established by Tony Richardson, John Osborne and Harry Saltzman which was responsible for producing many of the New Wave 'kitchen sink' films. He had made a modest name for himself during the 1960s as a producer with a liking for unconventional material, such as Lindsay Anderson's experimental short *The White Bus* (1966), as well as for possessing an eye for modish commercial properties like Richard Lester's *The Knack* (1965). Deeley and Baker took a joint producer credit on *Robbery*, with Bob Porter acting as production supervisor. Joseph Losey's son, Gavrik, was employed as a production manager. The film's director, Peter Yates, had previously worked with Deeley on the surreal comedy *One Way Pendulum* (1964) and had made his name with television series such as *The Saint*, as well as by directing *Summer Holiday* (1962), the popular vehicle for pop music star Cliff Richard.

The film is quite obviously based on the events of the Great Train Robbery which had captured media headlines in Britain earlier in the decade. The real-life criminals had stopped the Glasgow to London mail train on 8 August 1963 by tampering with signal lights and then relieved it of £2.3 million in used notes (the value of this today would be about £40 million). Thirteen of the gang were apprehended (three got away) after their fingerprints were found at their hideout on an isolated farm. They subsequently received very heavy sentences despite the fact that they didn't carry guns, although the driver of the train had been struck over the head with an iron bar. The robbers, who included Bruce Reynolds, 'Buster' Edwards and Ronnie Biggs, became celebrities via the press coverage and were seen in some quarters as folk heroes, working-class outlaws who had been given disproportionately long sentences because they were perceived to have snubbed their noses at authority. Much of this notoriety was an accident of timing, the robbery having caught the imagination of the public at a time when Britain's long-established class hierarchies were under attack from a new generation of young, aspirant working-class upstarts. Most of these, of course, did not become train robbers. The film follows the historical facts remarkably closely, with Baker's Paul Clifton standing in for Bruce Reynolds (who had masterminded the robbery) and James Booth, previously seen as Private Hook in *Zulu*, playing a dogged policeman based on Inspector Jack Slipper of Scotland Yard, who had pursued the real culprits relentlessly. The robbery itself is recreated in considerable detail, and the real-life escape from prison by Ronnie Biggs and his subsequent flight to Australia, and eventually Brazil, is mirrored in the final sighting of Baker arriving in America, having ditched his wife and avoided the fate of all his fellow gang members.

Robbery neatly continues the lineage of earlier Stanley Baker films such as *The Good Die Young, A Prize of Arms* and *The Criminal* in depicting a working-class lawbreaker in a sympathetic light. It also reflects a noticeable shift in both censorship and public attitudes. In the previous films, Baker's robber doesn't get away with it and is punished by death, but here he wins relatively easily, to the presumed enjoyment of the audience. Much of the film's pleasure lies in its careful accumulation of detail and in the meticulous sense of place. The location shooting by Douglas Slocombe is vivid and the direction by Peter Yates has real verve. As a former racing driver, it's perhaps understandable that he should handle the opening car chase through the busy London suburbs with such panache. Hollywood star Steve McQueen was so impressed that he hired Yates to direct one of cinema's finest car chases in *Bullitt* (1968). The underworld of London's gangland is depicted with a feeling of authenticity, as we follow the central characters from casinos and nightclubs, to shabby pubs and garages. Several scenes, such as those at a football match or of Baker jogging in the park, have a documentary quality to them. Baker adopts his familiar tone of self-contained, purposeful aggression. He is softly spoken but authoritative with his gang, even if his wife (Joanna Pettet) mockingly refers to him as 'the last of the great thinkers'. Audience empathy is encouraged by his adoption of a moral code; he tells his men 'No guns, no violence, no accidents – they (the police) don't use them and we don't need them.' It's a coolly understated, convincing performance, with the exception of what was to become the first in a series of unfortunate macho moustaches.

The immediate critical response was mixed. It received an award from the Writers' Guild of Great Britain for Best British Original Screenplay and most of the tabloid press were enthusiastic, with much praise for the opening chase sequence. Ernest Betts in *The People* described it as 'a masterly suspense film'. Others considered it a routine caper film hampered by the fact that audiences already knew what the ending would be. The characterisations were, quite fairly, criticised as being two dimensional. This was probably a consequence of having to disguise the film's link to the real events and individuals; the legal difficulties the film faced were reported in *The Times* in a piece entitled 'Film makers chase mail raid millions'. Baker is quoted as saying: 'We had to make sure there was no accidental identification with anyone. The characters in the film are in no way based on the characters who took part in the great train robbery.' Baker himself shared in the uneven notices, with Patrick Gibbs in the *Daily Telegraph* referring to him as 'just a walking moustache'. Nonetheless, its reputation seems to have held up rather better than these critics might have expected, with David Berry more recently acknowledging it as 'a well-crafted thriller'. Whatever the critics thought, the film was a major success at the British box office and got Oakhurst Productions off to a profitable start.

The making of the film produced some unusual press coverage. During post-production Michael Deeley had taken two of the rifles used in the film to the Mayfair gunsmiths Holland and Holland to sell them. The assistant who served him, one Reginald Taylor of Thornton Heath, decided that Deeley was a suspicious-looking character. He locked the door of the premises and called the police. The *Daily Mail* subsequently reported that Westminster County Court had awarded Deeley £100 in damages for wrongful imprisonment. Another story informed readers that Baker's intimate scenes with Joanna Pettet had actually been filmed at his family home in Wimbledon (no doubt to save money) in the bed that he usually shared with his wife. Meanwhile, the *Daily Express* took exception to a television interview Baker had given in which he suggested that the Great Train Robbery had not been an especially serious crime. He had argued that it was no worse than the money-making activities of big business or the eviction of an old lady by an avaricious landlord. The paper's columnist fumed that Baker's views were immature and hypocritical, pointing out to readers that Baker 'is not averse to a shrewd bit of money-making – having recently sold his house and site (which he bought for £7,500 a few years back) to the GLC for £69,000'. All publicity is good publicity, no doubt. Baker defended the film along similar lines in his later television interview with Clive James:

> I'm very proud to have been in and made *Robbery*. It was a good film. I think if you look at the picture closely the full message didn't get through to the audience, but there were a lot of injustices committed in my estimation with those people. I mean they were put away for 30 years – that's just awful – we tried to suggest that in the film.

He also defended his own sympathetic characterisation, telling James that if his character appeared 'dignified and clever' that's because he was in reality.

Baker's final film for Levine as actor and producer was *Where's Jack?* (1969), a costume romp set in the 1720s and based on the life of Jack Sheppard, a thief and jailbreaker who had become a folk hero with the poor of London. The film was shot in Ireland at Ardmore Studios and on location there, with Tommy Steele playing Jack and Baker cast as the film's ambiguous villain, the thief-taker Jonathan Wild. This time Baker produced alone for Oakhurst, with Bob Porter credited as his assistant and Michael Deeley as executive producer. In a press release, he explained his reasons for shooting in Ireland:

> I like the idea of being 'cut off' from the usual filming activity in Britain and America. It gives us a chance of being totally separate, isolated and basically 'alone'. It gives the actors and technicians a chance to think and work and talk about this one film for practically 24 hours a day, for months on end. You live and breathe the picture and your work benefits.'

It was an expensive production with a great deal of effort spent on achieving an authentic period look in the costumes, props and sets, under the supervision of designer Cedric Dawe. Large numbers of extras were employed, most notably for the spectacular final sequences of Jack's execution. Despite all of this, Ellen recalls a feeling of weariness during the shoot: 'Almost everybody involved in that film, even down to Tommy Steele, was making it to complete a contract of some form or another, so there was an atmosphere of just wanting to get it made.' She also felt that there was some confusion about who the film was aimed at and that it would have been better as a children's film.

The film's style is actually much closer to that of Tony Richardson's huge box office hit *Tom Jones* (1963), combining surface realism (seen in the depiction of London's muddy streets and starved urchins) with bawdy high spirits (lots of carousing in pubs and amply proportioned women in low-cut dresses). Perhaps this approach seemed outdated, as audiences stayed away and the critics were largely indifferent. Its comparative failure didn't encourage Levine to offer any further contracts to Oakhurst and, in any case, Baker's ambitions were developing in other areas of production by the end of the 1960s. The film isn't assisted by a repetitive plot structure in which Jack is trapped on several different occasions by Baker's character, only to repeatedly escape in ever more elaborate ways. With hindsight, the film is better than might be expected. It is handsomely produced, with evocative cinematography by John Wilcox and an effective score from Hollywood veteran Elmer Bernstein. Tommy Steele is engaging as Jack and the succession of dramatic set pieces, including an escape from prison via the sewers and a chimney flue, work well. Baker is suitably exaggerated as Wild, invoking memories of his villains of the 1950s such as Mordred in *Knights of the Round Table*. We first see him in silhouette, a darkly sinister figure, and he later holds court in his underground lair like some decadent crime lord. He is an embodiment of moral corruption, a man who makes a living catching thieves while operating a criminal empire of his own.

However, he retains some audience affection, maintaining a degree of ambivalence in the character. Before the impending execution, he allows Jack's lover to pay him one last visit and even confesses to seeing something of himself in the young outlaw. He seems only too aware that he is little different from the criminals he exploits, telling Jack: 'It's a wicked age, the only crime is poverty.'

The film is obviously intended as an entertainment but Baker knew that it was open to a more subversive political reading. If Jack Sheppard and Jonathan Wild are both the products of a corrupt society, then the only difference between them is that one resists this corruption while the other embraces it. Baker said of the film

> One of the attractions of the story for me is that Jack bucks this kind of corrupt authority cheerfully and enthusiastically – and if you look round today you can see just that kind of thing going on now. There are plenty of parallels between what went on in the eighteenth century and what goes on in this day and age.

This attempt to imbue a simple story with underlying social intentions chimes with what he was to tell Vincent Kane in their later interview about his motivations for moving into production.

Oakhurst's ventures spread beyond the films which Baker had been directly involved with himself as producer and star. While he busied himself with fulfilling the contract with Joseph Levine, Michael Deeley supervised two other films to completion. The first, *The Other People* (1968), which was also known as *Sleep is Lovely*, was a romantic melodrama made as a collaboration with producer Harry Field's Telstar company. Budgeted at just $60,000, it starred Peter and John McEnery as two brothers in love with the same woman, and featured Donald Pleasence and the young Bruce Robinson in its supporting cast. Paramount picked up the US distribution but the film virtually sank without trace. The same can't be said of Deeley's second solo effort for Oakhurst, *The Italian Job* (1969). Featuring Michael Caine and Nöel Coward, it was yet another caper movie featuring a gang of likeable rogues, this time out to steal a shipment of gold bullion under cover of the chaos caused by a football match between Italy and England. The film exploits the patriotism engendered by England's World Cup victory three years earlier and features a wonderful car chase through the crowded streets of Turin, with the gang driving red, white and blue Mini Coopers. With a witty script by Troy Kennedy-Martin and smart direction from Peter Collinson, it was an enormous commercial hit in Britain, where it still retains classic status among small boys of all ages. It caught the playful, optimistic mood of Swinging Britain just before the bubble burst at the end of the decade, and provided Oakhurst with another substantial payday. As an offshoot of his main operation, Baker also established Oakhurst Enterprises to film rock concerts for theatrical release. Two of these, featuring the bands Coliseum and Juicy Lucy, were released in 1970. Appropriately enough, Stanley's son Martin was later to produce television documentaries in the same area.

The press were quick to take an interest in this new face of Stanley Baker, the movie entrepreneur. An interview for *The Sun* in March 1970 headlined 'How sky-high Baker sees the valley now' refers to him as a 'film tycoon', although the reporter can't resist playing on his old tough guy image by picturing him as wearing a 'George Raft trench coat' and having the 'cocky assurance' of an Edward G. Robinson-style gangster. The term 'sky-high' was a reference to Baker's purchase (in partnership with Michael Deeley) in 1967 of Alembic House, a tower block on Albert Embankment where he installed his family and various friends (Richard Harris had the twelfth floor and *Zulu* composer John Barry lived with Jane Birkin on the tenth). From Baker's office on the eleventh floor he could survey the Thames and enjoy his uninterrupted, panoramic view of the Houses of Parliament. Ellen vividly recalls how he discovered the disused building while he was shooting *Robbery*. Ironically, the penthouse apartment now belongs to disgraced Tory politician Jeffrey Archer. For Bob Porter, who had known Stanley since the 1950s when he was still a supporting player and Porter was working as a stuntman, Baker's motivations were still essentially idealistic: 'He loved movies and wanted to make films that people would enjoy, but also ones that would get across a positive social message.' For Ellen, however, Stanley's metamorphosis into producer and businessman was not entirely welcome:

> I had married an actor, not a producer, but Stanley loved it. They were good years and he was full of optimism. He had a totally positive outlook about being a producer, but I think he suffered as an actor because he was so focused on producing. Other producers didn't always want to employ him as an actor in their films. He always wanted to keep working as an actor, but in the late sixties and early seventies he appeared in some poor films and his acting career suffered.

His production ventures were also an expensive, risky business and there is little doubt that this forced him, for financial reasons, into acting in films which were beneath his best work.

Among these were two made for the independent British producer Dimitri de Grunwald, *The Last Grenade* (1970) and *Perfect Friday* (1970). *The Last Grenade* is a largely disappointing film, despite a supporting cast which includes Richard Attenborough, Honor Blackman and John Thaw. It is a crude action-adventure movie, with Baker as a mercenary seeking revenge on the man who double-crossed him (played by the forgettable American actor Alex Cord). Despite location work in Hong Kong and a good deal of violence, the film generates little audience appeal or excitement. Baker's character is a surprisingly unsympathetic 'hard man' whose reasons for becoming a mercenary are never explained. In a plot which is never less than implausible, he has a temporary change of heart brought about by an unconvincing romantic affair with the wife of his boss. The cast look uncomfortable in their thinly developed roles, with the exception of Alex Cord whose performance is wildly exaggerated. The usually flat direction is subject to sudden bursts of frantic camerawork and jump cuts. Even the normally reliable Johnny Dankworth provides an overly emphatic score. The film is also uncharacteristically reactionary for Baker, with Cord's villain portrayed as a demented hippie in sunglasses and sporting long hair, contrasted sharply with the military sobriety of Baker's men. The promotional campaign for the film made typical use of Baker's established pedigree as a tough guy, citing his Welsh upbringing as an indication of his steely character. More interestingly, it also acknowledged his new status as a producer: 'Stanley Baker wears three hats – sometimes two at the same time. First he's an actor, secondly a producer and thirdly a television tycoon.' None of this hyperbole saved the film from critical and commercial oblivion.

Perfect Friday, although slight, is much more likeable. It is another in Baker's succession of caper films, although more overtly Swinging Sixties in its fantasy elements and visual styling than anything he had appeared in before. Baker is cast against type as Mr Graham, the seemingly straight-laced deputy under-manager of a bank, who secretly plans to rob his employer with the help of a jaded jet-set couple played by David Warner and Ursula Andress. Warner is Lord Dorset, a decadent, narcissistic aristocrat in need of money, while Andress is his glamorous, extravagant wife. Baker appears to have had a great deal of amusement making the film, despite his initial anxieties about Andress:

> I'd seen her about twice on screen and she'd been built up as a sort of 'body' and that was it. I really didn't look forward to working with her on that film, but having worked with her for about thirty seconds she was marvellous. First of all she is a good actress, she has a great sense of humour and she's extremely professional.

The filming allowed them to get to know each other intimately as they spent most of the first four days of shooting in bed together naked, providing plenty of footage for the numerous scenes of Andress in various states of undress which decorate the film. Ellen candidly remembers that they had the best sex of their married life on her husband's nightly return home from

107

the set! The film was helmed by the distinguished theatre director Peter Hall, who occasionally overindulges in fashionable stylistic tricks with freeze-frames and a complex editing structure which shuttles around in time. The film hints at the political undercurrents which were more obvious in *Robbery* and *Where's Jack*, as well as distantly recalling the gentle subversion of Ealing comedies like *The Lavender Hill Mob* (1951) in its depiction of the mild-mannered employee who bucks against authority. Here this is represented by the rigidly hierarchical world of the bank, but any wider resonance tends to be dissipated by the film's slightly tired 1960s trappings which have dated it.

The press response to the film was positive, even if few saw it as anything more than an exceedingly light entertainment. The tabloids, unsurprisingly, were mainly interested in the naked Ursula Andress, whereas the broadsheets were more concerned by the fact that a notable director like Peter Hall would make such an apparently throwaway film. John Russell Taylor in *The Times* seemed to feel that Hall had agreed to direct simply because the project would allow him the freedom to play around with technique. The notices for Baker himself were strong, with *The Sun* describing him as 'perfect in the role' and the *Daily Sketch* saying he was 'brilliantly and coolly clerical'. In a period when Baker was to take few genuinely satisfactory roles, it is an appealing performance. He brings a convincingly pedantic, officious quality to Mr Graham; sporting a bowler hat, thick-rimmed spectacles and a tightly-clipped moustache (the film's promotional posters turned him into a cartoon figure). This makes his transformation into thief and lover all the more enjoyable. Peter Hall was impressed and, according to Ellen, wanted Stanley to play the king in his production of *Hamlet*, as well as later offering him a part in his staging of John Osborne's *Watch it Come Down* with which he planned to open the National Theatre on the South Bank in 1976.

Baker's third acting appearance of 1970 was in *The Games*, which was produced by the London offices of Twentieth Century Fox and directed by a rising star of British cinema, Michael Winner. The film's ambitious, multistranded narrative follows the preparations of four athletes heading for the Olympic Games in Rome to take part in the marathon. Ryan O'Neal is the flashy American college boy who resorts to drugs to improve his chances and Charles Aznavour is oddly cast as a veteran Czech athlete returning for one last race at the behest of the communist authorities, while the unknown Athol Compton plays an Australian Aborigine who prefers to run barefoot. Baker is the obsessive coach of the British entrant, played by an ingratiating Michael Crawford as a former milkman whose talent is accidentally discovered when he is out doing his round. The film boasts beautifully photographed locations (Australia, Tokyo, London, Czechoslovakia) and there are smartly handled set pieces including an excitingly staged climactic race. It also manages to incorporate topical attacks on corruption in sport and the emergence of racial politics. On the negative side, the various plot strands are all predictable in their development, and national stereotypes, particularly of Australians, abound. Baker's role is a supporting one but it allows him to make an impression. In a throwback to *The Cruel Sea*, he is a manically driven bully. Disabled by an injury, he projects his frustrations onto Crawford's character and nearly kills him by pushing him towards an impossible two-hour finish time. His appearance, again wearing a bizarre moustache and glasses, adds to the disturbing aspect of the role. This is intensified by hints of repressed homosexuality as he forces Crawford to abandon the girlfriend who is distracting him from his running. It is an exaggerated performance but one that succeeds in drawing the audience's attention.

During this period he also returned to working in European based projects. These films could usually be relied on to provide him with a leading role and a reasonable pay cheque to invest in his ongoing production plans. *La Regazza con la Pistola/Girl With a Pistol* (1968) was an Italian production backed by Paramount, shot in English and Italian language versions. Monica Vitti, star of director Michelangelo Antonioni's European art house successes, plays a Sicilian woman who pursues the man who has 'dishonoured' her to London seeking her revenge, but is then diverted by the British doctor (played by Baker) who she falls in love with. A glossy black comedy, the film was a success in continental Europe, picking up a number of awards and nominations. These included a Best Actress prize for Monica Vitti at the San Sebastián International Film Festival and an Oscar nomination for Best Foreign Language Film at the 1969 awards. Despite this, the film was not given a theatrical release in the UK.

From the mid 1960s, Baker had also begun to work in television again on a regular basis. The majority of his performances were in one-off, single episode thrillers and crime dramas like *The Tormentors* (1966), which he made for the independent commercial company ATV. Here he played a political prisoner held in an unidentified European country, with James Mason as the psychiatrist who begins to sympathise with him. In the topical *A Fear of Strangers* (1964), also made for ATV as part of their *Drama '64* series, he is a corrupt, violent police inspector who tries to extract a false confession from a black murder suspect, while in *Fade Out* (1970), made by HTV for the *Saturday Night Theatre* slot, he is a television news reporter whose investigations reveal a government cover-up. In these parts he is always solidly reliable without ever extending his range greatly. There were also the inevitable celebrity appearances in light entertainment shows like *Secombe and Friends* (1966), where he got the chance to appear with two of his closest Welsh friends, Harry Secombe and Richard Burton, as well as the screening of a *Variety Club of Great Britain Challenge Match* (1967) where he and another old pal, Sean Connery, got to play golf with two professionals to raise money for charity. He provided the narration for Roger Graef's BAFTA-nominated *One of Them is Named Brett* (1965), a documentary short about the plight of the thalidomide children. *Who has Seen the Wind?* (1965) was a multinational television epic made for a series illustrating the work of the United Nations, in this case their role in helping displaced people and refugees. During the location shoot in Mazatlan, Mexico, Baker and his German co-star Maria Schell found themselves on board a ship when a hurricane hit. They had to be rescued, along with the rest of the cast and crew, by local fishermen in their boats.

Baker also appeared in several television dramas made in the UK or continental Europe by American companies. These included *After the Lions, Jackals* (1966) and *Code Name: Heraclitus* (1967), both made for the American series *Bob Hope Presents the Chrysler Theatre*. 'He enjoyed working for television', remembers Ellen, 'it drew on elements of film acting, in the way that you rehearse and then shoot, but as some of the broadcasts were live it also had the immediacy of working in the theatre.' The most memorable of his 1960s television appearances is also one of the briefest. In 1965 he appeared in TWW's *Return to the Rhondda*, an impressionistic documentary about the area where he grew up, presented by his fellow actor and friend Donald Houston, who had also grown up in the valleys. Baker is seen standing above the ruined remains of Ferndale's Number One pit, where his father had lost a leg and so many men had perished. His narration may be a touch sentimental, but it is also moving and deeply felt:

> This is a bad place. I struggled hard to keep out of this pit when I left school. For me there were two ways of doing it: through boxing or acting. It turned out to be acting – I liked acting, especially tough, heroic roles. The men who went down here were mostly tough men, men who lived dangerously and many of them were heroes.

The delivery is gentle and understated but carries an emotional weight lacking in most of his television work at this time.

He found a tidy way of combining his feelings for his roots with his growing entrepreneurial ambitions through his involvement with the television consortium HTV. Under government legislation, the franchise for producing commercial television in Wales and the west of England was held by TWW (Television Wales and West) from 1956 to 1968, with programme transmissions starting in 1958. Baker had actually appeared alongside Harry Secombe and Shirley Bassey in January 1958 in *The Stars Rise in the West*, a variety show which was the first programme broadcast by TWW. When the franchise came up for review and renewal in 1967, they found they had a powerful competitor in the newly established Harlech Television (later known as HTV). Baker became a major shareholder in the new company and one of its founding directors, along with the Burtons, Sir Geraint Evans, the actor David Hemmings, and the Conservative politician Lord Harlech, who led the company. With such glamorous backing and promising a line-up of star-studded drama, Harlech Television won the franchise and began broadcasting on 20 May 1968. With studios in Cardiff and Bristol, it quickly divided its operation to cover the two distinct geographical areas which it served, establishing HTV Wales/Cymru and HTV West. Baker remained a key figure behind the scenes with the company until his death.

Baker's career had now seen him progress from supporting actor to star to producer, then to running his own independent film production company and being on the board of a television consortium. The next logical step, or so it appeared to him, was to move up into the major league of British film producers, but this was a high-risk venture. The British film industry had, by the early 1960s, consolidated into what was effectively a duopoly consisting of the Rank Organisation and the Associated British Picture Corporation (ABpC). The industry's fortunes during the decade were buoyed up on a tide of American investment. When the bubble burst on American financial involvement in British filmmaking at the end of the 1960s, the domestic industry suffered a major crisis. Rank began gradually to withdraw from production, while ABpC's operation was taken over by the media giants EMI. The film industry began a process of fragmentation as audience attendance figures fell, cinema theatres closed, and production output plummeted. In interviews, Baker began to talk about his hopes for the renewal of filmmaking in Britain. In a press release issued by Oakhurst in 1969 he talks about the relative timidity of UK financiers in comparison with America:

> Often you're faced with misgivings by the people who put up the money to make the picture. They like to follow formulas. It's often so difficult to get a good picture, a picture that really means something, on the studio floor and actually start shooting it. I may be rather idealistic and optimistic, but I think that any picture *can* be set up and made; the distributors are there to be convinced. That's what is so fascinating about this business. So it's possible for anyone with enough guts to go to a big distributor and say 'Look, this picture is so bloody marvellous that it will make you a fortune.' If you can convince

them, then you can go ahead and make your picture. I've found in several cases that the American distributor is far more adventurous and willing to take a chance on an interesting property than an English one. The Americans are gamblers.

He went on to talk about the rigidity of the British production system, its lack of entrepreneurial flair, and the need to make films which look out to a wider, international audience in order to make them financially viable. His vision is of a company making entertainment films for a mass audience which nonetheless have something worthwhile and socially progressive to say. The example he cites, perhaps surprisingly, is that of producer Betty Box, who he had worked with in the late 1950s when unhappily contracted to Rank.

Unfortunately, Baker's faith in American producers proved to be overly optimistic as Hollywood began to implode in the late 1960s, consequently withdrawing its financial investment in British films. Talking to Clive James in 1972, he conceded that British filmmakers now had to look within the UK to find financial backing, but he still sounded optimistic: 'There's still a great future in the film industry in this country. We have everything in this country to make films. We have all the technical talent, we have all the actors, we have the directors, we have the terrain.' The difficulty remained in getting financial support within Britain to enable this talent to flourish now that the Americans were out of the picture. A rather more bruised Stanley Baker told Vincent Kane three years later that the future of the film industry actually lay in a closer working relationship with television, a statement which was remarkably prophetic considering the impact on British cinema in the 1980s of Channel Four. By that time he had experienced first hand how perilous the fortunes of a film producer working in Britain could be.

The eventual focus for Baker's ambitions to resurrect his native film industry turned out to be the production company British Lion. British Lion had been founded in 1927 and achieved moderate success during the 1930s and early 1940s. In 1945 Alexander Korda took a controlling share in the company and expanded its studios to include the facilities at Shepperton, but the company went rapidly into decline following several expensive box office failures and in 1948 it had to be bailed out with loans from the National Film Finance Corporation. By 1954 it had gone into receivership but was rescued again by loans from the NFFC, effectively becoming a nationalised film company. In 1957 it was put under the management of a board consisting of distinguished British filmmakers including the Boulting Brothers and Launder and Gilliat. As well as producing their own films, it frequently acted as a distributor for smaller independent companies and in the early 1960s backed some of the most notable New Wave films including *Saturday Night and Sunday Morning* (1960). Having become profitable, it was then sold off by the NFFC in 1964 to a consortium of the filmmakers it had supported (among them directors Tony Richardson and John Schlesinger), with Michael Balcon in charge. They couldn't stop the company from sharing in the decline which beset the whole industry in the late 1960s and early 1970s. By 1972 it was deep in the red, with the Shepperton facility running at a considerable loss. It was subsequently taken over by Barclay Securities who seemed more interested in trying to develop Shepperton for housing rather than filmmaking.

It was at this point that Baker and his two business partners, Michael Deeley and Barry Spikings, became interested in acquiring the company. Barry Spikings's background was in journalism and publishing where he had established himself in the 1960s as a rising star. While with the International Publishing Corporation (IPC) he had headed up their strategy to move into other areas of entertainment such as cinema. After leaving IPC, Spikings was looking for another way to pursue this ambition and found it by buying into the partnership which Baker had established with Michael Deeley. He also put his money into the purchase of Alembic House and the three of them founded a new company, Great Western Enterprises. Baker managed to secure Lord Harlech as another partner in this new venture. Their initial interest was in pop music, both making concert films and in backing festivals, but after an event at Lincoln was washed out by bad weather, with the loss of £200,000, they turned their attention to acquiring British Lion. This was to be achieved by becoming partners in Barclay Securities, with Alembic House used as the means to secure this. The building was sold, raising sufficient capital to buy a twenty-three per cent shareholding in Barclay Securities. Deeley and Spikings joined the board of British Lion, effectively taking over management of the studio. In Michael Deeley's words (as recounted to Alexander Walker), Stanley was 'primarily an actor-producer rather than a businessman, and lacking the rigorous discipline that Barry and I had decided was necessary to run British Lion, he wasn't involved in the day-to-day decision-making'. Baker always had serious doubts about risking the solid bricks and mortar investment represented by Alembic House but was seemingly persuaded by Barry Spikings. These anxieties were shared by Ellen who was personally opposed to the sale.

Things began well enough, with the revamped British Lion releasing a series of adventurous films including *Don't Look Know* (1973), *The Wicker Man* (1973) and *The Internecine Project* (1974), as well as a version of Ibsen's *A Doll's House* (1973) starring Jane Fonda. Admittedly, both *Don't*

Look Know and *The Wicker Man* had been commissioned by British Lion's previous management and Michael Deeley wasn't keen on either film, insisting on cuts for *The Wicker Man* and releasing the two films as a cut-price double bill. However, events rapidly took a bleaker turn when early in 1974 the British stock market suffered a collapse. British Lion's new parent company, J. H. Vavasseur (who had taken over from Barclay Securities), saw their share value plummet from 254p to 24p. Deeley and Spikings clung onto the wreckage as British Lion sunk into near oblivion, but poor Stanley Baker was washed away in the deluge. Barry Spikings initially became manager of a massively slimmed-down Shepperton operation, then he and Michael Deeley wrested control of British Lion's production wing away from Vavasseur and operated it briefly as an independent concern, making the films *Conduct Unbecoming* (1975) and *The Man Who Fell to Earth* (1976), the latter starring David Bowie. When EMI eventually took over in 1976, both Deeley and Spikings joined the board there. They were clearly hardened survivors in what had proved to be a pretty vicious business jungle; they later turned to producing films in America where they enjoyed some considerable success. For Baker, the venture was little short of a disaster. Apart from seeing his dreams for the British film industry in dust, it had cost him Alembic House, nearly bankrupted him, and derailed his acting career. Alexander Walker reported Michael Deeley as saying: 'Stanley Baker was furious and never forgave Barry and me for the whole "adventure". Every time I saw him, I could see him thinking, "Why didn't we keep our lovely safe building on the Embankment?"'

Ellen's fears about the nature of producing had been proved all too correct:

> Stanley met an awful lot of corrupt people when he went into producing. It was rife. There was the opportunity for all sorts of backhanders, if a producer was willing to hand out contracts for catering or cars to the right people. Stanley was absolutely straight. He had no time for anything underhand or dishonest, which didn't always make him the best person to work in that world.

For Bob Porter, there was a fundamental difference between Baker's approach to the film business and that of some in the industry: 'Stanley was interested in message films. He was idealistic, but there were others who were more concerned with the financial side of things. They saw it just as a means of making money.' He remembered how Stanley had helped Michael Deeley in the early days of Oakhurst when he had little money of his own. Such actions were indicative of his approach to business.

Through much of this trauma, Baker kept on acting in films, although the decline in his work was increasingly evident. *Una Lucertola con la Pelle di*

Donna/A Lizard in a Woman's Skin (1971) was the first of two further European co-productions he made in the early 1970s. The production involved companies from Italy, France and Spain, with Gala picking up the distribution rights in Britain and American International handling the American release (where it was marketed under the title *Schizoid*). The film belongs to the Giallo tradition in Italian cinema; 'giallo' being the Italian for 'yellow' and these films drawing their inspiration from the cheaply pro- duced detective novels published by Mondadori in predominantly yellow covers and bindings. The style was brought into Italian cinema by the director Maria Bava during the 1960s and perfected by Dario Argento in the 1970s, creating something of a cult following. The films typically combine a convoluted whodunnit plot with soft-core sex scenes and a generous helping of gory violence. *A Lizard in a Woman's Skin*, directed by Lucio Fulci, follows the formula closely, presenting a complex murder mystery in which the audience are led astray by a series of false leads before the dogged policeman finally uncovers the true culprit. The lurid plot development and weakly drawn characters are largely beside the point, as the film's focus lies mainly in its sensational aspects. British audiences were largely spared these as the film had six minutes cut by the censor. A recent American DVD release has made available the original Italian version which includes more explicit footage of the lesbian love scenes, further blood- thirsty detail of the central murder, and a grotesque sequence where the heroine finds some dissected, but still living dogs in a mental hospital. These shots led to a series of court cases in Italy brought by animal rights groups. They needn't have worried; the dogs were purely mechanical.

The film was promoted with American International's characteristic lack of subtlety. Their press book encouraged theatre managers to install dis- plays which illustrated the film's themes of psychological disturbance and split personalities, suggesting that they 'have local schools' psychology classes notified of the film'. If that didn't work, they could try a tie-in with travel agents to exploit the film's picturesque British locations which included Woburn Abbey. The press book also confusingly suggests that publicity should emphasise Baker's track record of playing villains, even though he plays the policeman here. The film gives Baker little to do; he doesn't appear until twenty minutes into the film. His police inspector is a cool-headed, imperturbable customer given to whistling tunefully while at work. His one flourish is his final speech when he unmasks the villain in traditional Agatha Christie style. Despite some overdirection involving distorted visuals, crash zooms, slow motion and shock cuts, the film fails to generate much excitement as the characters never resemble recognisable human beings. The multinational cast mouth their lines, only to be made more wooden-looking by the use of overdubbing. The film doesn't avoid unintentional hilarity, including the image of the leading lady pursued by a sinister, gigantic flying swan and Baker ordering his sergeant to round up every red-headed man in London. It does boast a score by Ennio Morricone and there is a vivid quality to the use of the English locations, but these can't disguise the crudely exploitative nature of the film, with sadistic violence (usually against women) presented as entertainment. Devotees of Giallo may find things to enjoy, but there are few rewards for a wider audience. A documentary included in the DVD release has an interview with Mike Kennedy, a Spanish pop singer who appears in the film as an unlikely hippie. He appears to have been on the receiving end of Baker's sense of humour during the filming. One can only assume Baker needed plenty of this to help him get through this production.

Worse was to follow with *The Twenty-One Carat Snatch* (1971), released in America as *Popsy Pop* and also known by the titles *The Butterfly Affair* and *Queen of Diamonds*. The film was a French–Italian co-production with location shooting in Venezuela. It was co-scripted by Henri Charrière, author of the bestselling novel *Papillon* and former inmate of the notorious French penal colony at Devil's Island. He also appears in the film as one of a gang of diamond thieves escaping through the South American jungle. Baker is the policeman pursuing them and Claudia Cardinale provides the love interest, but the film is a routine crime adventure hampered by poor production values, slow pace and incoherent plot development. It slid into commercial obscurity.

Baker's last feature film release for three years was to be *Innocent Bystanders* (1972), a British-made espionage yarn. It bears the all too obvious influence of the James Bond films, from its brassy score to numerous fight sequences and the use of colourful European locations. Unfortunately, the producers, Sagittarius (run by veteran producer George H. Brown), couldn't match the sort of budget that Eon Productions lavished on the Bond franchise. The result is a cheap-looking film with poorly staged stunts and a palpable lack of glamour. Peter Collinson, who had previously taken charge of *The Italian Job*, directs in a heavy-handed manner and James Mitchell, who had worked on *The Last Grenade*, provided the formulaic script. Although the plotline explains that Baker's character is a slightly faded, overaged secret agent making a last comeback, the 44-year-old Baker still looks ill at ease dealing with all comers in the fight scenes and his romance with Geraldine Chaplin lacks any spark. The film has an interesting support-ing cast, but both Donald Pleasence and Warren Mitchell are allowed to overact excessively. The film's tone is uncertain, veering disconcertingly between moments of knockabout farce and pretty unpleasant torture sequences. As a whole, it looks like a pale imitation of better thriller films. In earlier films, Baker was able to invest his tough guy roles with sympathetic qualities and contradictory elements of moral ambiguity which made them pertinent to the time, but here he is a stony-faced hard man, the part blatantly designed in the mould of more contemporary action stars like Clint Eastwood or Charles Bronson.

There is little question that by 1972 Baker's standing as an actor had fallen and, although still in regular employment as a weighty supporting performer and occasional lead, the standard of films he was appearing in was weak in comparison with his work of the late 1950s or the 1960s. It was inevitably difficult to keep playing tough guys as middle age became a reality; the possibility of stronger character roles, which films like *Accident* had promised, had faded away. His adventures as a producer had fallen foul of the ethics of a harsh business world where his, perhaps naive, idealism was unsuited. To his credit, he did leave a small slate of films as a producer which retain a great deal of cinematic interest, as well as enduring popularity. Nonetheless, having carefully built a career over the preceding twenty years, he now had to very nearly begin again. Final glory was to come, appropriately enough, in a return to his roots.

CHAPTER SEVEN

The Journey Home

With characteristic resilience, Stanley Baker's response to the turmoil of the early 1970s was to keep on working. Ellen confirms that there was never any question of declaring himself bankrupt or taking an easy way out of his situation: 'He was determined to pay any debts he had and to get back on an even keel. The only way to do that was to work, even if it meant taking parts in films he would rather not have done.' His last two roles in feature films were certainly not among the most distinguished or interesting of his career. *Zorro* (1975) was an Italian–French co-production, with Spanish locations standing in for Mexico. The cast and crew were largely Italian, with the French star Alain Delon taking the title role and Baker given second billing playing, as ever, the villain, Colonel Huerta. The film was acquired for release in America by United Artists but never found a British distributor and therefore didn't make it onto British cinema screens. Its lowly reputation wasn't helped by an initial release on video and then DVD which used a butchered American print with nearly forty minutes taken from its running time. In 2006 a nearly complete version was released on DVD in France which at least allows the viewer to get a better sense of what the film offered to audiences.

In retrospect, the film provides some pleasures. It is handsomely photographed, making good use of its attractive locations. A number of the fight sequences are well staged, particularly the immensely long final sword duel between Zorro and Huerta which is enjoyably grandiose. Unfortunately, these elements are countered by the slow pace and rambling plot (the cutting of the film for its previous sell-through release is partially understandable), as well as by some variable acting. Delon is dashing as the eponymous hero and Baker turns in a typical performance as the deceitful, conniving Colonel, awakening memories of the villains he played so frequently in the 1950s. However, he is given too little screen time to develop a convincingly menacing characterisation and is no match for the almost superhuman Zorro. Baker looks thin and drawn, which doesn't always make him believable in the action sequences. What really undermines the film is the jokey approach adopted by the filmmakers. Perhaps influenced by the recent success of Richard Lester's playful *Musketeer* films, the story is offered as pure camp; in one sequence Zorro's dog manages to unseat a whole troop of mounted soldiers before stopping off to urinate on a bush. The broad humour and pantomime performances, along with a jarring Europop theme song, dissipate any tension or excitement that the narrative might offer. This contrasts sharply with the recent Hollywood versions of this much-filmed story, starring Antonio Banderas and Catherine Zeta Jones, which kept the humour in check and consequently were more effective as adventure movies.

Baker's final feature film, *Pepita Jimenez/Bride to Be* (1975), is a dispiriting conclusion to his big screen career. A Spanish production featuring Sarah Miles and the young American actor Peter Day, it again failed to obtain a British theatrical release, although it had a limited run in America. Baker plays Don Pedro, a wealthy widower who courts Pepita Jimenez (Sarah Miles), a mysterious young woman whose rich, elderly husband has recently died. The courtship is scuppered when Pedro's estranged son returns home. He is a novice priest, but finds himself irresistibly attracted to Pepita with predictable results. The clichéd narrative unfolds at a painfully turgid pace and frequently shifts into florid melodrama, especially in the key sequences when Pepita confesses her feelings to her own priest and when Baker fights with his son. The happy ending where everyone is reconciled, with Pepita marrying Pedro's son with his blessing, is the stuff of soap opera. Sarah Miles appears distracted in her role and is often confined to dreamy long shots, most noticeably during the first forty-five minutes when she doesn't have a line of dialogue. The film's single point of interest is the striking similarity between Baker and the character he plays. Don Pedro is a wealthy man who enjoys the trappings of success (gambling at the casino, throwing lavish parties), but he is driven by a strong social conscience: he defies the other local landowners by paying his workers higher wages. Despite his privileged position, he has a relentless work ethic and a progressive outlook, believing that personal wealth must be justified by hard graft and that everyone deserves a chance to make a better life for themselves. Baker brings a greying charm to the role, but there is also a fragile quality about his appearance that lends his performance pathos.

The bulk of Stanley Baker's work in the mid 1970s, among it some of his most impressive acting for many years, was done for television. His first foray back onto the small screen was *Who Killed Lamb?*, a single play made for Yorkshire Television in 1973. It was subsequently given its first UK national screening as part of the second season of the popular ATV series *Thriller* on 16 March 1974. Baker plays yet another of his dogged police inspectors, this time investigating the murder of a 'saintly' businessman who is revealed to have been secretly operating as a blackmailer. If this was a relatively routine affair, *Graceless Go I* (first broadcast 8 October 1974) was more ambitious. Appropriately enough for Baker, it was made by HTV at their Bristol studios (the company of which he remained a director). He took the part himself having failed to persuade the original choice, Rex Harrison, to appear. It boasted an impressive cast including the Welsh actresses Rachel Roberts and Angharad Rees, as well as Ian McKellen and Peter Sallis. The script was by Anthony Storey, who would go on to write an impressionistic, book-length portrait of Baker in 1976. Storey visited the set during the shooting and developed the beginnings of a friendship with Stanley and Ellen. Despite Baker's strong connections with HTV and the fact that this was, by television standards, an expensive project, Ellen remembers that he was singularly unimpressed with their production standards during the recording of the teleplay. Storey's own account provides an interesting description of Baker at work:

> Once he is involved in the work he changes. He becomes the man he is playing. Even when he is not being used he may work at his part, doing whatever the person he is playing – an alcoholic doctor – would be doing in the real life situation [. . .] When he is called he is immediately in place and works with intelligent professionalism, openly sensitive to the needs of the director and his fellow-actors . . . This is what he enjoys. He loves acting.

Storey also gives a vivid account of the prickly relationship between Baker and McKellen during the production, as they clashed over politics.

If David Berry is correct in suggesting that Baker's 'most challenging roles from the late sixties on were in television', this really became apparent with the two projects he made for the BBC's prestigious *Play of the Month* slot. The first of these was *The Changeling*, an adaptation of the play by Thomas Middleton and William Rowley first performed in 1622. Recorded in late 1973, it received its first transmission on 20 January 1974. A strong cast, including Helen Mirren, Brian Cox and T. P. McKenna, were under the supervision of the experienced theatre director Anthony Page. Baker relished his role in this dark story of lust, betrayal and murder and his performance is sinister and intense. The production took him back to his early days at Birmingham Rep., giving him a chance to show audiences that he could still play classical roles. When asked on television about the challenge of playing such a role, he told Vincent Kane, with a rueful smile: '*The Changeling* was a chance for me to show, after many years of making movies, that I am really an actor.'

His second role for *Play of the Month* was a major success. *Robinson Crusoe* was screened on 29 December 1974 to Baker's best reviews for some years. The press heaped praise on James MacTaggart's direction and his faithful realisation of the novel's serious underlying themes, but it was Baker who was singled out for the greatest commendation. William Marshall in the *Daily Mirror* called him 'quite stupendous', while the *Daily Telegraph*'s reviewer said he had exactly 'the right drive and energy to express Crusoe's will to live'. The *Daily Express*, under the headline 'This highbrow Crusoe', described it as a 'virtuoso performance . . . brooding, melancholy, rarely letting a smile flit across his face'. Baker can have had few reviews in his career more complimentary than Shaun Usher's in the *Daily Mail*:

> Stanley Baker as *Robinson Crusoe* (BBC1) was a piece of casting so sound that it seemed inevitable, as soon as they announced it. For a character living alone for upwards of 20 years must be played by one of that small group of character actors who can dominate and deserve attention for hours at a time, without support. Along with Lee Marvin, Baker is the thinking man's toughie: manifestly dangerous in a brawl, yet just as evidently enjoying brisk activity above eyebrow level. These twin strands of personality held *Crusoe* together.

The BBC invested a sizeable budget on the production and consequently sold it to international markets as a standalone television film. It was screened to positive responses in America a month before its British transmission. The shoot was a demanding one, with Baker in virtually every shot, and can hardly have had a beneficial effect on his health. Glynne Morse's son, Gareth, remembers meeting Baker at this time and how immersed he was in preparing the role, his fascination with 'the attributes of creative and physical cleverness which enabled him to survive on his own. Of his intelligent comprehension of the character and life of the place and where Crusoe could get his food and shelter.' His characterisation is as determinedly resourceful as he was himself, but with his white beard and slightly bedraggled appearance, Baker also brought an air of melancholy to the part.

Leaving aside the obscure *Il Figlio Della Savana Orzowei* (1976), an Italian–German co-production made for television which was to be Baker's final screen credit, his last major role could hardly have been more fitting; he played Gwilym Morgan, the benign father in BBC Wales's adaptation of Richard Llewellyn's classic Welsh novel *How Green was my Valley*. Amid all the fluctuations of Baker's career, the importance of his Welsh roots remained a constant. In Anthony Storey's portrait of Baker he spends the best part of a chapter recounting a visit he made with him back to Ferndale. During the trip they encounter Baker's boyhood friend, Billy Rossiter, who shared two distinctions with Stanley: that of starting out as one of Ferndale's poorest sons; and of then becoming one of its most successful, having made himself a small fortune as a scrap merchant. Whatever romanticising takes place in Storey's account, it is clear enough how comfortable Stanley felt back on his old stamping ground. Ellen says that for him 'home' always meant Ferndale. He even named his racehorse 'Rhondda Prince'. In Ferndale there are still stories of his visits back home, of the pleasure everyone took in his success, and his lack of ego when he was among 'his people'. His sister Muriel compared his visits to Ferndale to the excitement he felt as a boy when the Sunday School made its annual daytrip to the seaside at Barry. For Peter Stead, this remains one of the most attractive features of Baker:

> What was most pleasing about his relationship with Wales was that it was entirely lacking in affectation. He was a poor boy from the Rhondda who had succeeded in London but who retained total respect and an enormous affection for what he had been given by his family and friends.

How Green was my Valley gave him the opportunity, all too rare in his career, to bring his feelings for his roots directly into his work.

Richard Llewellyn's original novel was written from a considerable distance to its subject matter by a man with, as Peter Stead puts it, 'little direct experience of Wales'. The BBC had previously made an adaptation in 1959, but popular memory tends to be dominated by the Hollywood film of 1941 directed by John Ford. This version has come in for criticism, a good deal of it warranted, for a lack of authenticity typified by the fact that of the major characters only Dai Bando is played by a Welsh actor (the cast consists mainly of Irish and English performers). As David Berry's detailed account of the film argues, it is better seen as belonging within the body of John Ford's work, with his characteristic love of frontier communities and homely tradition, than as reflecting much about the culture of south Wales. Much of the myth-making and romanticism of Ford's film derives from Llewellyn's novel and is still evident in the BBC's more restrained adaptations. However, a lack of authenticity is not a criticism that could easily be levelled at the version Baker appeared in. Adapted by Elaine Morgan and broadcast in six episodes from 29 December 1975 to 2 February 1976, it benefits greatly from a fine Welsh cast including Siân Phillips as the indomitable Mam, Nerys Hughes, Sue Jones-Davies, and Gareth Thomas as the village minister. In America it was broadcast as part of Twentieth Century Fox's *Masterpiece Theatre* slot and was sufficiently well received for Baker to receive an Emmy nomination as the Outstanding Lead Actor in a Limited Series.

Elaine Morgan's adaptation keeps the sentimentality mainly under control and the performances are assured, with memorable supporting work from the likes of Keith Drinkel as the fiery, politicised Ianto. The familiar representational clichés of south Wales are undeniably here, from the narrowmindedness of the Chapel to the gossiping women of the pit village, but there is enough that rings true to make the series moving on a number of occasions. Politically, the narrative is still cautious, presenting the callousness of the mine owners as being counterbalanced by the lack of judgement shown by the unions (who are indirectly responsible for Gwilym's death), but there is also much anger at the iniquities of an economic system that allows hundreds of men to be put out of work and into near starvation at the whim of Iestyn Evans (Jeremy Clyde), the new mine owner, who is exposed as a greedy ne'er-do-well, and a wife beater to boot. There is anger too at the suppression of Welsh culture, especially the Welsh language, as typified by a sadistic schoolmaster who beats any boy who dares to speak their native language. In an ironic twist, he is revealed to be a Welsh speaker himself who has suppressed his own identity in an attempt to 'better himself'. The progression of the narrative remains highly schematic, with characters required to carry a great deal of symbolic weight as each one represents various characteristics of life in south Wales at the end of the nineteenth century, but the quality of the acting manages to breath life into these roles.

This is particularly true in the case of Baker himself. In his career he rarely looked more at home in a role than he is here. Ellen explained to Anthony Storey why she felt Stanley's performance was so effective:

> He was playing his father. It's the first time he's had a chance to show that part of his own personality that is the result of the wonderful feelings he had . . . and still has for his father. You know, the archetypal Welsh miner and the kind of husband and father he is. So many people have said how marvellous Stanley was because he came off the screen, even though it was television, as their own father.

Gwilym Morgan is an embodiment of the values instilled into Baker in his own childhood, a role model of father and husband. He is kind and warmly affectionate, loyal to friends and family, traditionally masculine in his belief that a man must stand up for himself, and resolutely moral in the choices he makes. Only his conservative political views differentiate the character from Baker's own personality. His affinity with the part is evident in several scenes. There are echoes of Baker's success as an amateur boxer in the sequences where Gwilym encourages young Huw to learn how to box so he can defend himself against the bullies at school. There is a decidedly tongue-in-cheek exchange between Gwilym and Ianto about the superior wages and conditions enjoyed by English miners, during which Gwilym shouts 'I've never seen any good come out of England', only for Ianto to respond, with a sly nod to Baker's most famous role, 'I don't care whether they're English or Zulus.' Most movingly, when Huw has to abandon his hopes of university to work in the pit and bring in wages for the struggling Morgan household, his father tells him not to throw his life away, offering himself as an example of a wasted existence. It's hard not to feel that these are the kind of sentiments that Baker senior might have expressed to the young Stanley as he set out on his acting career.

The immediate critical reception of the series was mixed, perhaps because reviewers had recently experienced an overdose of Welsh television drama as *How Green was my Valley* followed on from ITV's productions of *The Stars Look Down* and *Sam*, both of which had Welsh settings. Some of these reviews from London-based critics are decidedly condescending in their attitude towards Welsh accents, but Baker's own notices are consistently impressive. Shaun Usher in the *Daily Mail* described both Baker and Siân Phillips as being 'appropriately strong and utterly at home in their roles'. Even Richard Last in the *Daily Telegraph*, who was initially sceptical of the sentimental clichés of the series, found himself won over by the last episode. Considering how seriously ill Baker was when he made the programmes, something which is visibly evident at times, it is hard not to see his performance as a final summation of his own values. It could hardly have been a more appropriate way to close his career, by paying tribute to the father who helped shape his life and who saw so little of the success that followed, but also, as Peter Stead puts it, because this role was 'truly an epitaph for his valley and all the other valleys too'.

During the 1970s, Baker's political leanings led him into a more direct involvement in party politics. In his television interview with Baker for BBC Wales, Vincent Kane asked him if he saw any contradiction in the fact that he was a wealthy man and also a 'dedicated socialist'. In reply, Baker refers first to his upbringing in Ferndale in the 1930s and how his personal experience of social injustice had left a lasting impression on him: 'If someone comes to me now and says you have too much money, why don't you share it around, I am quite prepared to. I am one of those actors who has not left this country; I pay my taxes here.' He talks with passion about the economic decline of the Rhondda and the need to provide assistance to the communities who live there. He also expresses regret that he had not been able to spend more time in south Wales to help with the people he sees as his own. In 1971 he provided the narration for *A Breed of Men*, a television history of the Miner's Federation scripted by Karl Francis and produced by HTV, which combines dramatised reconstructions, witness interviews and archival material in telling a heroic story of trade unionism in action. Even when he delivers his linking sections from his grand office in Alembic House overlooking Parliament and the Thames, there is no feeling that he is anything other than a genuine, committed representative for the working-class culture which made him, paying tribute to the men and women who were, for him, the real heroes.

A lifelong supporter of the Labour Party, Baker began to offer his assistance as the Wilson government sought, and failed, to obtain re-election in 1970. He took a central role in shaping their party political broadcasts for television, trying to add a greater degree of technical polish and providing voiceovers. He went on the road with Harold Wilson and spoke at rallies in south Wales during the 1974 election campaign that saw the return of a Labour government with Wilson restored as prime minister. Wilson later paid tribute to him:

> None in his profession had a greater social conscience. I remember his opening a general election campaign with me at Ninian Park, Cardiff a few years ago. It was his own speech, carrying forward his memories of poverty in a Welsh mining valley to create the message of today. It was a speech I have never forgotten . . . it was a message of sharing.

Ellen recalls seeing off an exhausted Stanley at the airport as he came straight from the conclusion of the campaigning to fly off for location shooting, bringing him daffodils from their garden. The election success was a cause for celebration for Baker, but the reward he was to receive appears to have come as a considerable surprise. In May 1976, as part of Harold Wilson's resignation honours list, Stanley Baker from Ferndale in the Rhondda found himself to be Sir Stanley. Although the grandeur of the knighthood seems to have caused some mirth in the Baker household, Ellen (now Lady Ellen) spoke of his happiness at the award: 'I feel he really deserves it, but he thinks of it as an honour for the valley and the film industry . . . he's so pleased, though of course he'd never admit it to a soul.'

He was to have precious little time to enjoy the honour. Looking at the film and television work that he completed in 1975, it is visible just how thin and tired Baker had begun to look. Alwyn Davies saw him in a Ferndale pub during the making of *How Green was my Valley* and was struck by how poorly he looked. It is easy with benefit of hindsight to notice how ill he appears in some of these later roles, and Baker himself may well have put his failing health down to the punishing workload he continued to maintain, as well as the strain he had endured during the British Lion debacle. He was not the kind of man to allow fatigue to stop him from doing the things that he wanted to. Or perhaps he was aware of how ill he was becoming but chose to push it to the back of his mind. Soon there was no disguising the situation and in late February 1976 the press reported that Baker had undergone an operation for cancer. His general weariness and the pain in his legs had finally led him to consult a doctor earlier that month and a subsequent X-ray revealed a spot on his lung. Speaking to journalists after his operation at London's Westminster Hospital (on the morning of his forty-eighth birthday), he confessed that he had always been a smoker, of cigars more lately, but managed to put a remarkably brave face on circumstances. The *Daily Mail* reported him as saying:

> It's great to be here – it's great to be alive. When they tell you first of all that you've got this thing it's a bit of a shock. It's very traumatic. I don't even like to use the word. But I've been through the operation and I'm out of hospital and I'm now going to concentrate on getting better.

He went on to thank the staff of the NHS hospital where he was treated and the hundreds of people who had sent him get-well messages. His decision to speak to the press about his illness had been influenced by Peter O'Toole, according to Ellen. He had witnessed Siân Phillips nursing O'Toole, who was recovering from cancer, during the making of *How Green was my Valley*. O'Toole suggested that the best policy was to be open with the media.

Anthony Storey went to visit the Bakers at their home in Spain in the early spring of 2006 and his memoir of Stanley provides a vivid, personal account of how Baker fought to recover from his operation and regain his health. He was on a course of chemotherapy to combat the disease and was frequently in considerable discomfort. Nonetheless, he continued to discuss future projects as an actor and, potentially, as a director, including the making of a sequel to *Zulu*. *Zulu Dawn* was eventually released in 1978 (although the original screenplay was written by Cy Endfield, he withdrew his involvement following Baker's death). He showed great bravery as he struggled to maintain the normal routine of his life, visiting friends, gambling at cards, going out to lunch. There were blood transfusions back in London to deal with the anaemia which occurred as a side effect of his drug treatments, and then further X-rays revealed the cancer had spread to his bones. Ellen recalls that in his final days his thoughts returned frequently to his childhood in Ferndale and that this seemed to bring him a great deal of tranquillity. His friend Harry Secombe sent him books of short stories and plays by Gwyn Thomas which depicted life in the Rhondda of the 1930s and Ellen remembers the pleasure he took in reading them. On his return to Spain, in characteristically bravura style, he decided to take a swim in his pool. Two days later his health had deteriorated such that he had to be taken to a local clinic. The Sunday newspapers in Britain reported that he had been admitted for suspected pneumonia the previous day and that two specialists were being flown out from Britain to see him. When they arrived that Sunday the decision was made to take him by ambulance to the Residencia Sanitaria Carlos Haya in Malaga where the facilities would be better. Nothing, however, could be done to halt his decline and he died late the following afternoon, 28 June 1976.

The obituaries paid warm tribute to his achievements. Characteristically, *The Guardian*'s was headed 'Tough guy from the valleys' and talked of him as being 'one of the first British actors with a working-class accent to become a film hero'. There was mention of his acumen as a producer and his involvement with the Labour Party, but the focus was mainly on the impact he had made on audiences as an actor who broke the mould in British cinema. There was also much comment on his loyalty to his Welsh roots, with Harold Wilson quoted as saying: 'His personality transcended even his talent. He retained and treasured his essential Welsh valley loyalties. Far from Wales, his loyalties to his own people never left him.' In her first press interview following his death, Ellen said:

> Our whole life together was filled with happiness. Even when he was ill he didn't let it spoil things. He'd make me laugh somehow and give me strength. He was a wonderful man. He loved Britain and he loved films. He was brave to the end and I know he would want me to be brave too. He would want me to be strong.

His death completed a dreadful year for the Baker family. His brother Frederick, who had spent his working life down the mines in south Wales, died earlier in 1976 after a long, painful fight with the lung disease pneumoconiosis. Not long before that their mother had also passed away after a brief illness. She was at least spared seeing the son she adored, and whose success had given her such pleasure, end his life so prematurely.

The most startling tribute paid to Baker came in the form of an obituary published in *The Observer* and penned by his friend of many years Richard Burton. The piece is a long, rambling, sometimes incoherent, sometimes poetic account of their friendship. It also a hymn to the working-class culture of south Wales which they had in common, expressed in language which veers from florid overstatement to images of haunting power. He describes Baker as 'tallish, thickish, with a face like a determined fist prepared to take the first blow, but not the second', and describes how Baker 'pelted the privileged as they came out of the grammar school because he was disallowed entry'. The latter comment is pure myth-making, but the article is often highly effective in placing Baker within the childhood landscape which had such a formative influence on him:

> Those low hills, those lowering valleys, the Rhondda Fawr, the Rhondda Fach, and their concomitant buses and grey roofs and pitheads and dead grass and crippled miners and cages endlessly falling with your father inside and

smashed to bits, and since with a convulsive heave Stanley shrugged off the mighty mountains and strode across Europe, who or what the devil killed him?

For an obituary, the article makes virtually no reference to any of the major events of Baker's life or to his achievements as an actor or producer. It also makes scant reference to either his marriage or his children, other than to refer to Ellen bizarrely as an 'exquisite alien'. The focus is on Baker as a product of the south Wales valleys: 'There is a class of Welshman, original and unique to themselves, powerful and loud and dangerous and clever and they are almost all South Welshmen and almost all from the Rhondda Valley.'

If this is overblown romanticising then it can be forgiven from someone who shared a similar background to Baker. What is less palatable is Burton's attempt to emphasise his own cultural status by pointing out the apparent intellectual failings of Baker: 'The lovely old Stanley wasn't exactly cultured. He read minds not books, he was harshly unpoetic, he didn't like people very much.' In response, Ellen describes how Stanley spent many of his spare hours reading, striving to provide himself with the education he never had in his early life. Viewing his television interviews with both Vincent Kane and Clive James would be enough to convince most that he was a thoughtful, articulate man. Burton's comments reveal more about his own pretensions than they do about Baker. Ellen was far from happy with the piece. The *Sunday Express* subsequently reported: 'Lady Baker, whose husband Sir Stanley Baker, died three weeks ago has been upset by an extraordinary article written by fellow actor Richard Burton.' The report refers to Burton's obituary as rambling and pretentious, and quotes Ellen as saying that Baker himself would have been amused by something so typical of Burton. The relationship between Baker and Burton had been long and sometimes close, but it had also been subject to tensions. It was the Bakers who had introduced Burton to his first wife, Sybil, and they had remained good friends with her even after her divorce from Burton. In later years, their careers took them in very different directions and their friendship was more distant. Ellen remembers how her children tried to ensure that she didn't see that Sunday's edition of *The Observer*, but the photographer Norman Parkinson came visiting that morning and brought the paper with him. Although she found the article upsetting, she recalls that as she sat in the garden reading it she was certain she could hear Stanley's voice laughing from the nearby willow tree.

The funeral, a private service for family and friends, took place early in July at Putney Vale Crematorium in London. Anthony Storey gives a slightly obtuse account of the occasion in his book, making much of the inadequate performance of the priest and archly refusing to name some of the famous individuals in attendance, such as the 'retired heavyweight boxer' (Henry Cooper), the Speaker of the House of Commons (George Thomas), and the 'Welsh actor' (Donald Houston) who read a poem. At the same time, his account of the grief of the young Glyn Baker is undeniably moving. Subsequently, Stanley Baker's ashes were scattered on the hillside at Blaenllechau overlooking his beloved Ferndale. An enormous crowd looked on, as a Welsh male voice choir sang. Among the throng was his old mentor and friend Glynne Morse. Near the close of the BBC's production of *How Green was my Valley*, Beth Morgan (Siân Phillips) says of her late husband, Gwilym: 'God will never let anyone go home until they have finished their stint.' Stanley Baker had finished his stint and come home.

Conclusion

It is now late November and I am driving up to Ferndale again. It's a dark, wild day with the wind whipping rain down the valley, as I make my way through the former pit villages into the Rhondda. BBC Radio Wales are broadcasting their afternoon programme from Ferndale Rugby Club and a plaque is to be unveiled in the Sir Stanley Baker lounge. We are commemorating the thirty years that have passed since Stanley Baker died. Lady Ellen is there, along with Stanley's sister Muriel, and all three of his sons. They have been joined by what seems to be half of Ferndale; the bar is packed to overflowing and there is laughter rolling out into the street. The comedian and broadcaster Owen Money is presenting the programme and attempting to keep some semblance of order, but he has a hard job on. The weather is so awful that the live radio transmission has been abandoned. The interviews are being recorded instead for broadcast on Monday. The local choir performs and one of its members sings solo. It's a warm, joyful scene and one can imagine how much Stanley would have enjoyed it himself.

Ellen is telling affectionate stories about Stanley. She has been talking to one of the BBC crew who can remember accidentally meeting him as a child on a visit to London. He was shooting *Perfect Friday* and she still recalls his kindness and how pleased he was to discover she was from south Wales. Muriel is astounding everyone with her precise memory for Ferndale and its inhabitants. Glyn, Stanley's second son, has been bowled over by the affection he has encountered today. He talks about what a unique place this is and what determination it took for Stanley to drive his way from here to success. He remembers how, at his own wedding, Stanley's great childhood friend Billy Rossiter has been invited but then felt so uncomfortable on the day that he couldn't come in from outside. Stanley, by contrast, never felt at a disadvantage to anyone. Adam, who is similarly overwhelmed by the occasion, reflects on the difficulties of being raised with a famous father and the challenge all the children faced in making their own way in the world from under his shadow. This event itself is a remarkable testimony to how much Stanley Baker still means to the people here in Ferndale.

Many of the stories told are of Baker the private man. They return repeatedly to his loyalty to this place and to the kindness he showed to people when he was out of the public gaze. Muriel remembers how Stanley provided the deposit for the first pub which she and her husband ran, as

130

well as how he helped them to buy their first house. She recalls how he paid for their brother Freddie's daughter to go to Vienna to train as a singer. He always regretted that while he had escaped to a better life, it was Freddie who remained and worked down the pit. When his brother became ill he helped to support him. Muriel says: 'He was the most generous man you ever met. He always looked after people.' She always remained close to Stanley, spending one of her two weeks' annual holiday from the pub with him. Similarly, Glynne Morse's son Gareth told me of Stanley's loyalty and gratitude towards his father, remembering the occasion he discovered him at his father's bedside when Glynne was in the Bristol Eye Hospital.

Ellen has many stories in the same vein. She recounted how, after his death, she was going through his papers and discovered a cheque book which she had never seen before. It detailed a series of payments he had made over the years to various people who had come asking for his help. They included out-of-work actors, friends down on their luck, and even Henry Cooper's old manager. She remembered these people coming to see Stanley over the years but had no idea that he was helping them in this way. For her, what was typical of Stanley was not so much the generosity, but the fact that he didn't want anyone to know what he was doing, not even her. Another story takes her back to 1970 and the making of *The Last Grenade* on location in Spain. Stanley leapt out to stop a car which was heading down the wrong side of the road. Behind the wheel, to his amazement, he found none other than Daphne Rye, the casting agent who had discovered the young Baker and signed him up for Tennants, the agents who also handled Richard Burton. He hadn't seen her for fifteen years but they soon got talking and he ended up giving her the money to set up her new business in Spain, a kind of bar cum library which he became a frequent patron of afterwards.

As well as the private kindness, there is the loyalty to his childhood roots. His son Martin reflected on the impact of that upbringing in Ferndale:

> The influence of his background never left him. He always remained at heart a working-class Welshman. He kept the same friends for years and was always drawn to people in the film crew who shared his background to some degree. He loved boxing, pubs and gambling. He was always a Labour-voting socialist. His sense of ambition came from his background. If you didn't want to work down the mine, you got out. He was able to walk both sides of the line, talking to aristocrats or working-class crew members. He was always himself and people accepted him for that.

His cousin John Wyatt said of him: 'I don't think he ever forgot where he came from. It was always a part of him. He was proud of his background and I know the people of the valleys were always proud of him.' Siân

Phillips, in an interview for Steve Freer's affectionate BBC documentary on Baker, remembered going on a journey to the valleys with him during the making of *How Green was my Valley* and realising that:

> He was adored by everyone and, in a funny sort of way, he was the one who hung on to his roots more. Although his career was international and he lived abroad and lived in London, there was something about Stanley that never did leave the valleys and that, of course, was very attractive and people sensed this.

A section of the BBC's website covering south east Wales includes a discussion board where people can attach their views or memories of Baker. A number come from people currently living in south Wales who continue to feel a direct connection to him. One says: 'While I was growing up in Ferndale in the Rhondda, Stanley Baker was my hero. A 'boy from the valley' who managed to avoid the colliery and become an international star.' Another describes him as 'a proud part of the Rhondda's heritage'.

The press had always been attracted to the story of a poor boy making good and many of his press cuttings over the years return to this theme. The other angle that they were often fascinated with was of how the on-screen tough guy was in private a tender, loyal family man. Back in 1965, *Showtime* magazine was delighted to inform its readers about his 'soft side'. The evidence they give for this comes in the form of his comments about Ellen: 'I could stand losing everything I had gained materially without getting suicidal, but losing Ellen would really finish me. I just can't imagine life without her.' Six years later, with his twenty-first wedding anniversary to celebrate, he told another magazine: 'There's no formula for a happy marriage. We stay married because we still want to live together.' One only has to see Ellen talking about Stanley now, thirty years after his death, to see how much they meant to each other and how that love has continued.

The comments on the BBC's web pages offer fascinating evidence as to his continued popularity with fans. There are those who want to acknowledge his talents as an actor: 'Stanley Baker was a consummate film actor, as effective at portraying "hard men" as he was in his more sensitive roles.' Another praises his performance in *Accident*: 'His Oxford don Charley is a masterpiece of acting [. . .] Bogarde plays Bogarde, and does it as well as ever. But Stanley acts him off the screen. It's Stanley's film.' As flattering as these comments are, there is something else here. It is not so much Baker's acting as his screen image which has made the lasting impression on audiences. One says: 'There is a certain magnetism about Stanley Baker – when he is on screen with other actors, it is always him you are watching', while another suggests that the only reason for watching a routine film like *Hell Below Zero* is to see Baker. One comment says simply that he was 'an actor of great screen presence'. These descriptions suggest something other than just acting ability at the core of Baker's appeal. In his book *Stars*, Richard Dyer tries to define the nature of 'charisma' which is so central to our understanding of screen stardom. For Dyer, this aspect of stardom is not some magical, inexplicable occurrence, but a synthesis of the star's own intrinsic qualities, the historical context in which they appear, and the inclinations of the audience. It is evident from the BBC's website that Baker's impact is indicative of this combination of elements.

It's worth considering the estimation of Baker made by other commentators. Anthony Storey's account of him frames his life by focusing almost entirely on his final days and the legacy of his early years. Storey is concerned principally with Baker the working-class hero and in examining the influence of his upbringing. He spends little time looking at Baker the actor, star or producer. As a result, he too easily buys into the myth of Baker the 'hard man'. Although recognising the determination which drove him from those valleys to success, he assumes that the sense of 'threat' which gave his screen performances their edginess was a true reflection of the inner man. This underestimates both Baker's abilities as a performer and the vulnerability which often made his tough-guy roles interestingly complex. Peter Stead's short essay on Baker celebrates his Welshness (justifiably enough), but is sidetracked by unhelpful comparisons between Baker and Richard Burton. Stead accepts the prevailing mythology of Burton as an intellectual and artist, crediting Baker's commercial success to his more pragmatic, career-minded approach. He contrasts Burton, with his 'poetic love of language', somewhat disparagingly with Baker, whose acting is a matter of natural instinct rather than the studied skill of Burton. Again, there is an assumption that achieving this naturalness on screen involves no conscious effort, as well as an unwillingness to recognise that the power of film stardom lies in the performer's ability to represent something which is relevant and meaningful to their audience. It's difficult to accept the image of an uneducated, inarticulate man which both accounts present. There may have been few books in the family household of the young Baker but, as Ellen recounts, Stanley was an avid self-improver who read voraciously as an adult. Anyone who has seen footage of his interviews with Vincent Kane and Clive James will have trouble recognising the man of limited vocabulary and simple thoughts described by Storey. Instead they will see a lively, keen intelligence at work, and a man whose choice of words was measured and expressive.

Other accounts of Baker take fuller account of his achievements as an actor and his appeal as a star. For David Berry, Baker was Britain's first 'authentic virile working-class screen hero', who paved the way for a new generation of proletarian stars. But he was also a subtle actor who could suggest the inner tensions in his characters, an ability which made him 'for almost two decades one of the most compelling of British male performers'. Julian Upton's essay on Baker, 'The outsider', provides a balanced comparison with Burton which recognises that 'in many ways Baker had a more effective on-screen presence than Burton, and, in retrospect, he seems to have contributed more to the British cinema of the 50s and 60s'. He also recognises the complexities achieved by Baker in his roles for Joseph Losey, especially in *Accident*. Other film historians, examining stardom in the kind of terms described by Richard Dyer, have sought to place Baker in his historical context in order to gauge his meaning for audiences. For Geoffrey Macnab, it is the Celtic qualities of both Baker and Burton which made them so startlingly different in the staid British cinema of the 1950s. In contrast with the ineffable 'niceness' of Rank's roster of contract players (mainly English), Baker and Burton 'were truculent and self-destructive [. . .] notions of loss, disappointment and betrayal are central to any understanding of their careers and how they managed to become stars.' At a time marked by youth rebellion and a disillusionment with Britain's ruling elite, these 'valley boys' were the outsiders who could give voice to these feelings of unrest. Andrew Spicer also acknowledges Baker's tough-guy roles of the late 1950s as a symptom of the social unease of the period and a forecast of the changes that were to occur in the class landscape of 1960s Britain. He points out how these roles helped establish the figure of the anti-hero in British cinema, the man of honour who is forced to use questionable methods for a worthy cause. This analysis also sits well with some of Baker's later roles in films like *The Last Grenade* and *Innocent Bystanders* where the dangerous edge of his earlier persona has hardened into a more vengeful figure. These later characterisations can be seen to chime with the mood of cynicism which typified British culture in the early 1970s, as the optimism of the 1960s faded.

Beyond the specifics of the historical background which helped make Stanley Baker a star, there is something more. This can be found in his screen roles and the persona created in the media, but also in the life of the private man. Baker was a star whose public image was often a projection of the values he held personally. This quality had much to do with that upbringing in the south Wales valleys and the working-class family and community to which he belonged. It includes some contradictions, not least of which is that the background which forged his talents also drove him away in his pursuit of success. This was a source of regret and was partly expressed in his abiding generosity to others from similar backgrounds. The quality which made him loved included a sense of grievance, an anger which spoke to the personal experiences of many of his fans, but just as important was the warmth and generosity which made him a romantic figure, as well as an archetypal tough guy. Baker was that rare thing, an authentic screen hero.

Bibliography

Babbington, Bruce (ed.), *British Stars and Stardom* (Manchester: Manchester University Press, 2001)

Berry, David, *Wales and Cinema: The First Hundred Years* (Cardiff: University of Wales Press, 1994)

Bragg, Melvyn, *Rich: The Life of Richard Burton* (London: Hodder & Staughton, 1988)

Brown, Allan, *Inside the Wicker Man: The Morbid Ingenuities* (London: Sidgwick and Jackson, 2000)

Caine, Michael, *What's It All About?* (London: Random House/Arrow, 1992)

Caughie, John and Kevin Rockett, *The Companion to British and Irish Cinema* (London: BFI/Cassell, 1996)

Caute, David, *Joseph Losey: A Revenge on Life* (London: Faber & Faber, 1994)

Chapman, James, 'Our finest hour revisited: The Second World War in British feature films since 1945', *Journal of Popular British Cinema*, no. 1, 1998

Chibnell, Steve and Robert Murphy (eds), *British Crime Cinema* (London and New York: Routledge, 1999)

Ciment, Michel, *Conversations with Losey* (London: Methuen, 1985)

Clay, Andrew, 'Men, Women and Money: Masculinity in Crisis in the British Professional Crime Film 1946–1965', in Steve Chibnell and Robert Murphy (eds), *British Crime Cinema* (London and New York: Routledge, 1999)

Curran, James and Vincent Porter (eds), *British Cinema History* (London: Weidenfeld & Nicolson, 1983)

Davies, John, *A History of Wales* (London: Penguin, 1994)

Dyer, Richard, *Stars* (London: BFI, 1998)

Elsom, John, 'Baker, Sir (William) Stanley (1928–1976)', in the *Oxford Dictionary of National Biography* (Oxford: Oxford University Press, 2004)

Gardner, Colin, *Joseph Losey* (Manchester and New York: Manchester University Press, 2004)

Geraghty, Christine, 'Masculinity', in Geoff Hurd (ed.), *National Fictions* (London: BFI, 1984)

Gillett, Philip, *The British Working Class in Postwar Film* (Manchester: Manchester University Press, 2003)

Girelli, Elisabetta, 'Transnational maleness: The Italian immigrant in *Hell Drivers*', *Cinema Journal*, vol. 44, no. 4, 2005

Hall, Sheldon, 'Monkey Feathers: Defending *Zulu*', in Claire Monk and Amy Sergeant (eds), *British Historical Cinema* (London and New York: Routledge, 2002)

BIBLIOGRAPHY

——*Zulu – With Some Guts Behind It: The Making of the Epic Movie* (Sheffield: Tomahawk Press, 2005)

Hill, John, *Sex, Class and Realism: British Cinema 1956–1963* (London: BFI, 1986)

Jones, Gareth Elwyn, *Modern Wales: A Concise History* (Cambridge: Cambridge University Press, 1994)

Junor, Penny, *Burton: The Man Behind the Myth* (London: Sidgwick & Jackson, 1985)

Laing, Stuart, *Representations of Working Class Life* (London: Macmillan, 1986)

Ledieu, Christian, *Joseph Losey* (Paris: Edition Seghers, 1962)

Lester, David and Jhan Robbins, *Richard and Elizabeth* (London: Arthur Baker, 1977)

MacFarlane, Brian, *The Encyclopedia of British Film* (London: Methuen, 2003)

Macnab, Geoffrey, 'Valley boys', *Sight and Sound*, vol. 4, no. 3, March 1994

——*J. Arthur Rank and the British Film Industry* (London and New York: Routledge, 1994)

——*Searching for Stars: Stardom and Screen Acting in British Cinema* (London and New York: Cassell, 2000)

Marwick, Arthur, *British Society Since 1945* (London: Penguin, 1996)

——*The Sixties* (Oxford: Oxford University Press, 1998)

May, John, *Rhondda 1203–2003: The Story of Two Valleys* (Cardiff: Castle Publications, 2003)

Milne, Tom, *Losey on Losey* (London: Secker & Warburg, 1967)

Monk, Claire and Amy Sergeant (eds), *British Historical Cinema* (London and New York: Routledge, 2002)

Murphy, Robert, *Sixties British Cinema* (London: BFI, 1992)

Murphy, Robert (ed.), *The British Cinema Book*, (London: BFI, 2001)

Phillips, Siân, *Public Places* (London: Hodder and Stoughton, 2001)

Robertson, James C., 'The censors and British gangland, 1913–1990', in Steve Chibnell and Robert Murphy (eds), *British Crime Cinema* (London and New York: Routledge, 1999)

Shail, Robert, 'Stanley Baker's "Welsh western": Masculinity and cultural identity in *Zulu*', *Cyfrwng*, vol. 1, 2004

——*British Film Directors: A Critical Guide* (Edinburgh: Edinburgh University Press, 2007)

Spicer, Andrew, 'The emergence of the British tough guy: Stanley Baker, masculinity and the crime thriller', in Steve Chibnall and Robert Murphy (eds), *British Crime Cinema* (London and New York: Routledge, 1999)

Typical Men: The Representation of Masculinity in Popular British Cinema (London and New York: I. B. Tauris, 2001)

Stead, Peter, *Acting Wales: Stars of Stage and Screen* (Cardiff: University of Wales Press, 2002)

Storey, Anthony, *Stanley Baker: Portrait of an Actor* (London: W. H. Allen, 1977)

Upton, Julian, 'The Outsider', *Planed/Planet*, no. 150, 2002

Walker, Alexander *Hollywood, England* (London: Orion, 2005)

——*National Heroes* (London: Orion, 2005)

OTHER SOURCES

Stanley Baker gave two important television interviews towards the end of his career which have been used in compiling this book: first, with Clive James for *Cinema*, recorded on 6 October 1972 and broadcast by Granada Television on 2 November 1972 (a full transcript is held in the special collections of the British Film Institute); then, secondly, with Vincent Kane for *Kane on Monday*, BBC Wales, 1975.

A good deal of fascinating material, including many interviews with family and colleagues, is contained in Steve Freer's documentary portrait, *Stanley Baker: A Life in Film*, first broadcast by BBC Wales on 28 June 1996 to commemorate twenty years since Baker's death. The programme was repeated as part of the BBC Wales series *The Silver Screen* in November 1998.

Some of the DVD reissues of Baker's films include fascinating bonus materials including interviews, documentaries and promotional shorts. Of particular interest are the special edition of *Hell Drivers* (Carlton), *The Guns of Navarone* (Columbia TriStar) and *Zulu* (Paramount).

Filmography

(d. = director; sc. = scriptwriter; ph. = cinematography; pd. = production design; m. = music; p. = producer)

1. *Undercover* (1943)

d. Sergei Nolbandov; sc. John Dighton and Monja Danischewsky; p. Michael Balcon for Ealing
with John Clements, Tom Walls, Michael Wilding, Godfrey Tearle, Rachel Thomas, Niall MacGinnis and Finlay Curry.

2. *Obsession* ((1949)

d. Edward Dmytryk; sc. Alec Coppel; p. Nat A. Bronsten for GFD/Independent Sovereign
with Robert Newton, Sally Gray, Phil Brown and Naunton Wayne.

3. *All Over the Town* (1949)

d. Derek Twist; sc. Derek Twist and Michael Gordon; p. Ian Dalrymple for Wessex
with Norman Wooland, Sarah Churchill, Cyril Cusack, Bryan Forbes and Patrick MacNee.

4. *Your Witness* (1950)

d. Robert Montgomery; sc. Hugo and Ian Butler; p. David E. Rose and Joan Harrison for Coronado
with Robert Montgomery, Leslie Banks, Felix Aylmer, Harcourt Williams and Michael Ripper.

5. *Lilli Marlene* (1950)

d. Arthur Crabtree; sc. Leslie Wood; p. William Gell for Monarch
with Lisa Daniely, Hugh McDermott and Russell Hunter.

6. *The Rossiter Case* (1951)

d. Francis Searle; sc. Kenneth Hyde, John Hunter and Francis Searle; p. Anthony Hinds for Hammer
with Helen Shingler, Clement McCallin and Sheila Burrell.

7. *Cloudburst* (1951)

d. Francis Searle; sc. Francis Searle and Leo Marks; p. Anthony Hinds for Hammer
with Robert Preston, Elizabeth Sellers and Colin Tapley.

8. *Captain Horatio Hornblower RN* (1951)

d. Raoul Walsh; sc. Ivan Goff, Ben Roberts and Aeneas Mackenzie; p. Raoul Walsh
for Warner Brothers–First National
with Gregory Peck, Virginia Mayo, Robert Beatty, James Robertson Justice and
Christopher Lee.

9. *Home to Danger* (1951)

d. Terence Fisher; sc. John Temple-Smith and Francis Edge; p. Lance Comfort for
New World
with Guy Rolfe, Rona Anderson and Francis Lister.

10. *Whispering Smith Hits London* (1951)

d. Francis Searle; sc. John Gilling; p. Anthony Hinds for Hammer
with Richard Carlson, Greta Gynt, Herbert Lom and Dora Bryan.

11. *The Cruel Sea* (1953)

d. Charles Frend; sc. Eric Ambler; p. Leslie Norman for Ealing
with Jack Hawkins, Donald Sinden, John Stratton, Denholm Elliott, Virginia
McKenna, Moira Lister, Megs Jenkins and Glyn Houston.

12. *The Red Beret* (1953)

d. Terence Young; sc. Richard Maibaum and Frank Nugent; p. Irving Allen and
Albert R. Broccoli for Warwick
with Alan Ladd, Leo Genn, Susan Stephen, Harry Andrews and Donald Houston.

13. *Knights of the Round Table* (1954)

d. Richard Thorpe; sc. Talbot Jennings, Jan Lustig and Noel Langley; ph. Frederick A.
Young; p. Pandro S. Berman for MGM
with Robert Taylor, Ava Gardner, Mel Ferrer, Anne Crawford, Felix Aylmer, Robert
Urquhart and Niall MacGinnis.

14. *Hell Below Zero* (1954)

d. Mark Robson; sc. Alec Coppel and Max Trell; p. Irving Allen and Albert R. Broccoli for Warwick
with Alan Ladd, Joan Tetzel, Basil Sydney, Jill Bennett and Niall MacGinnis.

15. *The Good Die Young* (1954)

d. Lewis Gilbert; sc. Vernon Harris and Lewis Gilbert; p. Jack Clayton for Remus/Romulus Films
with Laurence Harvey, Gloria Grahame, Richard Basehart, Joan Collins, John Ireland, Margaret Leighton and Robert Morley.

16. *Beautiful Stranger* (1954)

d. David Miller; sc. Robert Westerby and Carl Nystrom; p. Maxwell Setton and John R. Sloan for Marksman
with Ginger Rogers, Jacques Bergerac and Herbert Lom.

17. *Richard III* (1955)

d. Laurence Olivier; sc. Laurence Olivier and Alan Dent (adaptation); ph. Otto Heller; pd. Roger Furse and Carmen Dillon; m. William Walton; p. Laurence Olivier for London Films
with Laurence Olivier, John Gielgud, Ralph Richardson, Cedric Hardwicke, Claire Bloom, Patrick Troughton and Michael Gough.

18. *Helen of Troy* (1956)

d. Robert Wise; sc. John Twist and Hugh Gray; ph. Harry Stradling; m. Max Steiner; p. Robert Wise for Warner Brothers
with Rossana Podesta, Jacques Sernas, Cedric Hardwicke, Harry Andrews, Niall MacGinnis and Brigitte Bardot.

19. *Alexander the Great* (1956)

d. Robert Rossen; sc. Robert Rossen; ph. Robert Krasker; p. Robert Rossen for United Artists
with Richard Burton, Fredric March, Claire Bloom, Harry Andrews, Danielle Darrieux, Michael Hordern, Niall MacGinnis and Peter Cushing.

20. *A Child in the House* (1956)

d. C. Raker Endfield; sc. C. Raker Endfield; p. Benjamin Fisz for Golden Era/Eros
with Phyllis Calvert, Mandy Miller, Eric Portman and Dora Bryan.

21. *A Hill in Korea* (1956)

d. Julian Amyes; sc. Ian Dalrymple, Anthony Squire and Ronald Spencer; p. Ian Dalrymple for Wessex Films
with George Baker, Harry Andrews, Michael Medwin, Robert Shaw and Michael Caine.

22. *Checkpoint* (1956)

d. Ralph Thomas; sc. Robin Estridge; p. Betty Box for Rank
with Anthony Steel, Odile Versois, Maurice Denham, Michael Medwin and James Robertson Justice.

23. *Hell Drivers* (1957)

d. C. Raker Endfield; sc. C Raker Endfield and John Kruse; ph. Geoffrey Unsworth; p. Benjamin Fisz for Aqua/Rank
with Herbert Lom, Peggy Cummings, Patrick McGoohan, Jill Ireland, William Hartnell, Wilfred Lawson, Sidney James, Alfie Bass, Gordon Jackson, David McCallum and Sean Connery.

24. *Campbell's Kingdom* (1957)

d. Ralph Thomas; sc. Robin Estridge; p. Betty Box for Rank
with Dirk Bogarde, Michael Craig, Barbara Murray, James Robertson Justice, John Laurie and Sidney James.

25. *Violent Playground* (1958)

d. Basil Dearden; sc. James Kennaway; p. Michael Relph for Rank
with Anne Heywood, David McCallum and Peter Cushing.

26. *Sea Fury* (1958)

d. Cy Endfield; sc. Cy Endfield and John Kruse; p. Benjamin Fisz for Aqua/Rank
with Victor McLaglen, Lucianna Paluzzi, Gregoire Aslan, Robert Shaw and Barry Foster.

27. *The Angry Hills* (1959)

d. Robert Aldrich; sc. A. I. Bezzerides; ph. Stephen Dade; pd. Ken Adam; m. Richard Rodney Bennett; p. Raymond Stross for MGM
with Robert Mitchum, Elisabeth Mueller, Gia Scala, Leslie Phillips and Marius Goring.

28. *Blind Date* (1959)

d. Joseph Losey; sc. Ben Barzman and Millard Lampell; ph. Christopher Challis; m. Richard Rodney Bennett; p. David Deutsch for Sydney Box/Independent Artists/ Rank
with Hardy Kruger, Micheline Presle, Robert Flemyng and Gordon Jackson.

29. *Jet Storm* (1959)

d. Cy Endfield; sc. Cy Endfield and Sigmund Miller; ph. Jack Hildyard; p. Steven Pallos for Pendennis/British Lion
with Richard Attenborough, Hermione Baddeley, Bernard Braden, Diane Cilento, Harry Secombe, Sybil Thorndike, Mai Zetterling, Marty Wilde, Megs Jenkins and Glyn Houston.

30. *Yesterday's Enemy* (1959)

d. Val Guest; sc. Peter R. Newman; ph. Arthur Grant; p. Michael Carreras for Hammer
with Guy Rolfe, Leo McKern, Gordon Jackson, Richard Pasco, David Lodge and Bryan Forbes.

31. *Hell is a City* (1960)

d. Val Guest; sc. Val Guest; ph. Arthur Grant; p. Michael Carreras for Hammer
with John Crawford, Donald Pleasance, Maxine Audley, Billie Whitelaw and Warren Mitchell.

32. *The Criminal* (1960)

d. Joseph Losey; sc. Alun Owen; ph. Robert Krasker; m. Johnny Dankworth; p. Jack Greenwood for Merton Park/Anglo-Amalgamated
with Sam Wanamaker, Margit Saad, Patrick McGee, Gregoire Aslan, Murray Melvin, Nigel Green and Jill Bennett.

33. *The Guns of Navarone* (1961)

d. J. Lee Thompson; sc. Carl Foreman; ph. Oswald Morris; m. Dimitri Tiomkin; p. Carl Foreman for Columbia
with Gregory Peck, David Niven, Anthony Quinn, Anthony Quayle, James Darren, Irene Papas, Gia Scala, James Robertson Justice, Richard Harris and Bryan Forbes.

34. *Sodom and Gomorrah* (1962)

d. Robert Aldrich; sc. Hugo Butler; pd. Ken Adam; m. Miklos Rozsa; p. Gottfredo Lombardo for Titanus (Italy)/Pathé (France) in association with Joseph E. Levine
with Stewart Granger, Anouk Aimee, Pier Angeli and Rossana Podesta.

35. *Eve* (1962)

d. Joseph Losey; sc. Hugo Butler and Evan Jones; ph. Gianni di Venanzo; m. Michel Legrand; p. Robert and Raymond Hakim for Interopa (Italy)/Paris Films (France)
with Jeanne Moreau, Virna Lisi and Giorgio Albertazzi.

36. *A Prize of Arms* (1962)

d. Cliff Owen; sc. Paul Ryder; ph. Gilbert Taylor; p. George Maynard for Inter-State/British Lion
with Tom Bell, Helmut Schmid, John Westbrook and Patrick Magee.

37. *In the French Style* (1962)

d. Robert Parrish; sc. Irwin Shaw; p. Robert Parrish and Irwin Shaw for Cassanna/Orsay/Columbia
with Jean Seberg, Phillipe Fouquet and Jack Hedley.

38. *The Man Who Finally Died* (1963)

d. Quentin Lawrence; sc. Lewis Greifer and Louis Marks; ph. Stephen Dade; p. Norman Williams for White Cross/British Lion
with Peter Cushing, Mai Zetterling, Niall MacGinnis, Nigel Green and Eric Portman.

39. *Zulu* (1964)

d. Cy Endfield; sc. John Prebble and Cy Endfield; ph. Stephen Dade; m. John Barry; p. Stanley Baker and Cy Endfield for Diamond Films/Paramount
with Jack Hawkins, Ulla Jacobssen, James Booth, Nigel Green and Michael Caine. Foreword spoken by Richard Burton.

40. *Dingaka* (1965)

d. Jamie Uys; sc. Jamie Uys; p. Jamie Uys for Embassy/Paramount
with Juliet Prowse, Ken Gampu and Siegfried Mynhardt.

41. *Sands of the Kalahari* (1965)

d. Cy Endfield; sc. Cy Endfield; ph. Erwin Hillier; m. Johnny Dankworth; p. Cy Endfield and Stanley Baker for Pendennis/Paramount
with Stuart Whitman, Susannah York, Nigel Davenport, Theodore Bikel and Harry Andrews.

42. *Accident* (1967)

d. Joseph Losey; sc. Harold Pinter; ph. Gerry Fisher; pd. Carmen Dillon; m. Johnny Dankworth; p. Joseph Losey and Norman Priggen for London Independent Producers
with Dirk Bogarde, Jacqueline Sassard, Michael York, Delphine Seyrig and Vivien Merchant.

43. *Robbery* (1967)

d. Peter Yates; sc. Edward Boyd, Peter Yates and George Markstein; ph. Douglas Slocombe; p. Michael Deeley and Stanley Baker for Oakhurst/Avco Embassy/Paramount
with James Booth, Frank Finlay, Joanna Pettet and Barry Foster.

44. *La Ragazza con la Pistola/Girl With a Pistol* (1968)

d. Mario Monicelli; sc. Rodolfo Sonego and Luigi Magni; m. Ennio Morricone; p. Gianni Hecht Lucari for Documento Film (Italy)/Paramount
with Monica Vitti, Carlo Giuffre, Corin Redgrave and Anthony Booth.

45. *Where's Jack?* (1969)

d. James Clavell; sc. Rafe and David Newhouse; ph. John Wilcox; pd. Cedric Dawe; m. Elmer Bernstein; p. Stanley Baker for Oakhurst/Paramount
with Tommy Steele, Fiona Lewis, Dudley Foster, Sue Lloyd and Alan Badel.

46. *The Last Grenade* (1970)

d. Gordon Flemyng; sc. Kenneth Ware; ph. Alan Hume; m. Johnny Dankworth; p. Josef Shaftel for Dimitri de Grunwald/Cinerama
with Alex Cord, Honor Blackman, Richard Attenborough, Andrew Keir, Julien Glover, Ray Brooks and John Thaw.

47. *The Games* (1970)

d. Michael Winner; sc. Erich Segal; ph. Robert Paynter; p. Lester Linski and Michael Winner for Twentieth Century Fox
with Michael Crawford, Ryan O'Neal, Athol Compton and Charles Aznavour.

48. *Perfect Friday* (1970)

d. Peter Hall; sc. Anthony Greville-Bell and C. Scott Forbes; ph. Alan Hume; m. Johnny Dankworth; p. Jack Smith for Dimitri de Grunwald/Sunnymede
with Ursula Andress and David Warner.

49. *Una Lucertola con la Pelle di Donna/A Lizard in a Woman's Skin* (1971)

d. Lucio Fulci; sc. Lucio Fulci, Roberto Gianviti, Jose Luis Martinez Molla and Andre Tranche; m. Ennio Morricone; p. Edmondo Amati for Apollo Film (Italy)/Films Corona (France)/Atlantida Film (Spain)
with Florinda Bolkan, Jean Sorel, Anita Strindberg, Alberto de Mendoza and Leo Genn.

50. *The Twenty-One Carat Snatch/Popsy Pop* (1971)

d. Jean Herman; sc. Henri Charrière and Jean Herman; p. Gisele Rebillon for Sofracima/Audifilm (France)/Fida Cinematografica (Italy)
with Claudia Cardinale, Henri Charrière and Georges Aminel.

51. *Innocent Bystanders* (1972)

d. Peter Collinson; sc. James Mitchell; p. George H. Brown for Sagittarius
with Geraldine Chaplin, Dana Andrews, Donald Pleasence, Sue Lloyd and Warren Mitchell.

52. *Zorro* (1975)

d. Ducio Tessari; sc. Giorgio Arlorio; p. Luciano Martino for Mondial Te F. I. (Italy)/Les Productions Artistes Associés (Paris)/United Artists
with Alain Delon, Ottavia Piccolo, Enzo Cerusico, Moustache and Adriana Asti.

53. *Pepita Jimenez/Bride to Be* (1975)

d. Rafael Moreno Alba; sc. Rafael Moreno Alba; p. Emaus
with Sarah Miles, Peter Day and Eduardo Bea.

FILMOGRAPHY

Baker also appeared in the short film *The Tell-Tale Heart* (1953), which was written and directed by J. B. Williams for Film Alliance, and provided the narration for *One of Them is Brett* (1965), a short documentary directed by Roger Graef for the Society for the Aid of Thalidomide Children.

Baker's production company Oakhurst were responsible for making *The Other People* (1968) and *The Italian Job* (1969), both produced by Michael Deeley.

TELEVISION

Stanley Baker took part in a number of television productions; the following is a brief list of his more substantial appearances.

Choir Practice (1952, BBC)
The Taming of the Shrew (1952, BBC)
The Creature (1955, BBC)
Jane Eyre (1956, BBC)
The Squeeze (1960, BBC Wales)
Return to the Rhondda (1965, TWW)
Fade Out (1970, HTV)
The Changeling (1974, BBC)
Robinson Crusoe (1974, BBC)
How Green was my Valley (1975–6, BBC Wales)

Index